This World
of Dreams

This World of Dreams

Richard Quinney

Borderland Books

Copyright ©2014 Richard Quinney. All rights reserved. No part of this book may be reproduced in any form without written permission from the publisher, with the exception of brief excerpts for review purposes.

Published by Borderland Books, Madison, WI
www.borderlandbooks.net

Publisher's Cataloging-In-Publication Data
Quinney, Richard.
  This world of dreams / Richard Quinney. — 1st ed.
  Includes bibliographical references.
  ISBN: 978-0-9835174-5-0

1. Quinney, Richard — Philosophy. 2. Farm life — Wisconsin — History. 3. Wonder (Philosophy) 4. Future life. 5. Reality. I. Title.

PS3567.U53 T45 2014

818.6   2013917201

Printed in the United States of America
First edition

Thus shall ye think of all this fleeting
  – *The Diamond Sutra*

Contents

Preface 7

One	A Lifetime Lived 9
Two	Some Work of Noble Note 12
Three	A World of Dew — and Yet 13
Four	These Letters and These Photographs 15
Five	And Much Abides 19
Six	A Family Farm 23
Seven	We Shall Not Cease from Exploration 26
Eight	Out of Ireland 28
Nine	A Handful of Things I Know 33
Ten	As Long as We Are Remembered 39
Eleven	A Spiritual Life 46
Twelve	The Visual World 54
Thirteen	The Written Word 57
Fourteen	Transcendent Dreams 61
Fifteen	Lovely, Dark, and Deep 65
Sixteen	Our Days and Nights Together 69
Seventeen	Nothing Is Lost 75
Eighteen	I Shot an Arrow into the Air 77
Nineteen	The Teller of Tales 83
Twenty	When We Were Cowboys 86
Twenty-One	I Thought about You 91
Twenty-Two	The Leisure of an Elderly Present 95

Twenty-Three	The Way of Everyday Life	*97*
Twenty-Four	Field Notes	*102*
Twenty-Five	Narrow Road to the Interior	*107*
Twenty-Six	When Words Come	*122*
Twenty-Seven	Once Upon a Summertime	*132*
Twenty-Eight	Our Revels Now Are Ended	*143*
	Illustrations	*145*
	Bibliography	*147*

Preface

THE DIAMOND SUTRA of the Mahayana tradition begins with the phrase "Thus I have heard." The Buddha had been walking with the monks at the end of day, and sat down to rest. An elder monk named Subhuti asked the Buddha a question. What follows is a dialogue regarding perception of reality. The teaching is about the unlearning of preconceived notions of the nature of reality. At the end of the Diamond Sutra is the famous four-line verse:

> Thus shall ye think of all this fleeting:
> A star at dawn, a bubble in a stream,
> A flash of lightning in a summer cloud,
> A flickering lamp, a phantom, and a dream.

I have thought about and contemplated the nature of reality for as long as I can remember. Beginning on the farm, walking the land, working in the fields, tending the farm animals, and listening to the soft words of my family as the darkness folded us into the night. And we would dream ourselves into another day.

One
A Lifetime Lived

IT IS MAY. The year is 2012. This is how I am living my life. This is what I am doing with my life. Elizabeth Hardwick begins her book *Sleepless Nights* this way. Although she writes it as a novel, she gives the protagonist her own name. The book demonstrates the illusory nature of the distinction between fiction and nonfiction. Any story of a life is created and transformed as soon as the author's words are written on the page. What is not a work of fiction? A dream dreamed again at the break of day. The author and the subject of the story are of shared identity.

New leaves are forming on the trees surrounding my house in town. At the farm, Dear Father and Mother, the land is being prepared for another year of crops. The chicken house is gone, the stanchions have been removed from the barn, another farmer is herding heifers and steers, and acres of land are allotted to the growing of vegetables. And a new farm couple is living in the house you built when you were married nearly a century ago. I drive to the farm occasionally to see the beauty of the land, marsh, and wooded hills, as the seasons come and go. To give a prayer of thanks for the life you lived and the life you made and gave. With me, you are in this world — in mind and body and spirit — living still and still living.

Letter home, 1956. I have held my first college class. As I rode the "El" to the downtown campus of Northwestern University, I realized that this evening could make or break my hopes for a teaching career. There were moments of fright as I entered the lecture hall and made the long walk to the lecture table. Professor Kimball Young had given me instructions for administering the examination that would precede my lecture on population. Talking was much easier than I had expected. I guess the secret is to be excited about your subject. After class several students came up front to say that my lecture was very interesting. No need to tell you how this made me feel. The evening is over and I know that at last there is something I can do. It is past midnight and time for bed. I look forward to seeing you on Sunday.

Lexington, Kentucky, 1964. It is evening and we are at the Holiday Inn at the edge of town. We are sitting around a table, friends at the university, watching and listening to J. D. Crowe and his band. She leans toward me and whispers under the bluegrass music that I am more a "Richard" than an "Earl." From then on I will know myself by the middle name given to me at birth. To family and childhood friends I still will be known by my first name, and only comfortable with that. To anyone who will know me after that night at the Holiday Inn, with the music of J. D. Crowe, and the advice of a friend, I will be "Richard." Would that our lives be long enough to be known by many names.

Letter, 1958. Dear Earl. Your letter came this morning and needless to say it was a surprise as you gave us no inkling of it when you were home a couple of weeks ago. We did think it probably would happen but not quite so soon I guess. After all you'll be 24 and should know what you want. It's a mighty serious step and we hope you have considered everything, and everything will be fine and you'll be very happy. We hope we won't lose our son. The wedding plans sound very nice, so much nicer than a big affair and glad it's a church wedding.... As Ever, Mom.

Over half a century has passed since I broke the news. My leave taking from one life, the one I had known from the beginning, to the one that has stretched to time present. A career of teaching, the good fortune of two daughters, the moves from one place to another, books and photographs, a marriage that lasted twenty-nine years and then ended, a happy courtship and remarriage, retirement, several ailments and diseases, and the coming of another summer. This could be a dream. And a lifetime lived.

Two
Some Work of Noble Note

DAILY DECISIONS of things to be done. Often as a melancholy figure casting an eye to another shore. Like Homer's hero yearning for fresh travel after returning to beloved Ithaca. Tired and aging but seeking to explore, brief as that may be. Think of yourself as Ulysses in Tennyson's poem:

> Old age hath yet his honor and his toil;
> Death closes all: but something ere the end,
> Some work of noble note, may yet be done,
> Not unbecoming men that strove with Gods.

In the morning as the hour hand of the clock edges to seven, the bedroom begins to lighten. I will turn seventy-eight this month—a fortunate man, I know. Hardly a morning passes without my thoughts going back to the farm of my beginning. I imagine the great bur oak standing tall in the field, always a solace and a reminder that old age has its honor. And I imagine that I am looking across the field to the old place of my ancestors. Any sorrows or laments are tempered by my thankfulness for this life. Songbirds are calling, mating, and nesting. I wonder what the day will bring. Might there be some work of noble note.

Three
A World of Dew—and Yet

IN A CHINESE SUTRA we are told that what is true never vanishes. What does vanish when we are mindfully aware is delusion. Delusions, illusions, and dreams are in a realm beyond conscious awareness in our moment-by-moment daily lives. The Diamond Sutra proclaims that creations of the mind are like dreams, phantoms, and bubbles. Can the mind ever break out of its dream state? Let's say, at least, that being mindfully aware alters our dreams. Whether the alterations bring us closer to what is true is a question beyond our human ability to answer.

Content I am to imagine myself as the keeper of a diary, much like the simple pastor in Georges Bernanos's novel *The Diary of a Country Priest*. Writing down things not always told to parishioners, recording thoughts and observations, and being ambivalent about the writing. But always the diarist who would not, could not, do otherwise.

If our lives are the stuff of dreams, if the mind even in awareness can never know the truth, the truth of our existence, the truth of daily reality, then what are we to do? Maybe the same as we would do if we knew the truth, could know the truth; we would live carefully and with great compassion. It could be that in not knowing we are even more careful and compassionate in the living of our everyday lives. Living without certainty of the truth makes our living more precious and meaningful. Each moment is a moment filled with the meaning that we give to our actions and to our thoughts — the meaning that we create in our daily relations with others, near and far. In not knowing, I am who I am.

Kobayashi Issa, author of the haibun spiritual journal *The Spring of My Life,* wrote this poem two hundred years ago:

This world of dew
Is only the world of dew —
And yet...and yet...

Yes, and yet. How to live with life as a dream? These lines could well serve as the theme for my journal as novel. One goes on living carefully and with wonder. And with thankfulness.

Four
These Letters and These Photographs

THESE MANY LETTERS and photographs stored in boxes and in the drawers of chests and buffets, and resting in attics and in the basements and in the closets of aging houses. Occasionally someone will browse a family album and try to learn more about an ancestor. How many times have I been one of these explorers of family history, hoping to know about those who lived a long time ago?

I know there is a difference between the words written in a letter and what I read now after the passing of the writer. There is a difference between the portrait of the ancestor living at the instant of the photograph and my viewing of the portrait after the ancestor has passed away. An aura surrounds the words and images of those now gone.

And there is the realization that there is a fine line, and only a fine line, between those who once lived and those of us who live today. And the separation between the living and the dead vanishes readily with time. The vastness of our time of being unborn makes our living, our existing, but a drop of dew, a flash of lightning, and a dream. Unborn is our primary natural state. These letters and these photographs are reminders of our brief lives of being among the born. Our messages remain for a while.

You asked in your letter for advice on whether to stay or leave. How many times have I asked this question? Perhaps the theme

runs through the lives of us all. The larger issue being: How should I live my life? Looking back on a life — a life in retrospect — you see clearly what was only glimpsed as life was being lived. Does it make any sense to lament what could have been otherwise? To think about the actions and deeds that could be changed if given the chance to relive that former time? Life — this life of dreams — is lived presently even as patterns and memories of the past and visions of the future shape it. The privilege of retrospect is possible only after the fact of the living. Retrospect is a thought, a moral critique, an abstraction, rather than real life. With compassion, toward others and ourselves, we know that we are living our daily lives the best we can. Likely you are about to plant your garden as the soil absorbs the rains that came in the night.

A friend recently sent me a quotation from the Woody Allen movie *Crimes and Misdemeanors* spoken by Professor Levy, a sage philosopher. Giving advice on how to view our lives in retrospect, he says, "We are all faced throughout our lives with agonizing decisions. Moral choices. Some are on a grand scale. Most of these choices are on lesser points. But! We define ourselves by the choices we have made. We are in fact the sum total of our choices." The sum total, I will remember that. How we have lived in the whole course of our given time is the record of our human attempt to find meaning in an otherwise unknown universe. And that meaning for us is the sense that we have done the right thing as often as possible. That our lives have been in the direction of what is good and true, good and true as far as we can know.

Look at these letters and these photographs of those who have lived and gone before us. See the faces and read the words of those of long ago, some remembered and some forgotten and some now without name.

Five
And Much Abides

PEN AND PAPER, often all that is needed. With paper and pen you seek to resolve the contending forces, giving balance to loss and gain. When Maurice Sendak died recently, someone recalled his saying, "I cry a lot because I miss people. They die and I can't stop them. They leave me and I love them more."

Solace, of sorts, in the philosophy of Lucretius: Death is only the dispersal of atoms. We all are connected, and when we die our atoms join other atoms in the universe. Live by the simple law — seek happiness and avoid pain. Shed the twin delusions of fearing what we cannot avoid and desiring what we cannot have. Step off the wheel and accept existence as it is. This surely brings a sense of wonder, rather than gloom and resignation. All is transitory: contemplate this unceasingly. Embrace beauty and the pleasures of the world where they may be found. Equanimity with pen in hand.

After a reading of his poem about the Holy Grail, Tennyson was heard to say, "Yes, it is true. There are moments when the flesh is nothing to me, when I feel and know the flesh is the vision, God and the spiritual the only and true — depend upon it, the spiritual is the real, it belongs to me more than hand and foot." Tennyson spoke of himself as being of the Eternal Reality, saying that the spiritual "is the only true and real part of me." We are told that a silence fell on the party for some time after the poet left the room. The shades on the tall windows of the living room have been opened. I am seated at the table this morning reading the responses I gave in an interview a sociologist friend recently conducted with me about the state of my health.

> *The last time we met there was the hip problem, of whether to have hip replacement surgery. There was the risk that because of chronic leukemia, and because of the brain hemorrhage that I had several years ago, I would have a higher risk of death during surgery. I have delayed surgery, but I have considerable pain and walking is difficult. I'll wait and see the orthopedic surgeon next year.*

> *But another factor has come into my decision-making. About a month ago, I went to hospital emergency for a day. It was decided I was not having a heart attack. But I ended up after that day with atrial fibrillation. I had an echocardiogram about a week later, and it was found that I have an aneurism on my aorta. I then met with a cardiac surgeon about a week later. He told me not to worry immediately, that aneurisms sometimes develop as we age. I am to see the cardiac surgeon in a year's time to determine if the aneurism has increased in size. So there's no reason for cardiac surgery now. But there is the added information that hip surgery would be even riskier because of the cardiac problem. The decision about hip surgery has been superseded by other health conditions.*

As you age, you think more about living with the conditions that you are presented with, rather than trying to cure them. The philosophical, the existential, question is mortality itself. I'm more interested in staying alive than trying to correct a disability. I would like to go for long walks in the woods and photograph, go to the mall and walk, and travel to foreign countries. But my primary sense of well-being is in the work that I do daily. And in my daily relationships with friends and family. I don't feel a disability as long as I have energy and mind, and find spiritual and mental satisfaction in my life.

You ask, "Do you ever, outside of thinking about your family and your loved ones, think about your professional legacy, ever?" I don't think about it in terms of worrying about it. I think what will be will be. And I'm not emotionally involved in thinking about it. Although I must say I have a certain confidence. It's part of the mystery, you know. All will pass in the grand scheme of things. The world of art and literature is now my reference, and it is to this world that I hope to contribute my verse. And one has little control over where one will be placed in that. And to me that's not the issue. The issue is how I am living now. This to me is more important than whether or not there is a legacy.

Tennyson has the old Ulysses standing on the shores of the island. A melancholy figure still yearning for more adventures. The day is waning, and Ulysses calls out to his friends, saying that it is not too late to seek a newer world. And finally there is the urgency of the last sentence of Tennyson's poem on the life of Ulysses:

Though much is taken, much abides; and though
We are not now that strength which in old days
Moved earth and heaven, that which we are, we are;
One equal temper of heroic hearts,
Made weak by time and fate, but strong in will
To strive, to seek, to find, and not to yield.

Much abides each day as we make our way slowly across landscapes old and new.

Six
A Family Farm

Sometime ago, long after the creation of a universe and a galaxy and a planet that would be called Earth, natives roamed this continent without claim to land. Eventually, we as emigrants from other lands made the land our own. We cleared and tilled and farmed the land. We built our buildings — houses, barns, granaries, and sheds for livestock and machinery.

Four generations lived on this farm in Walworth County. The farm was made of many families, connected by marriages and births, as it slowly grew during the years. Pioneer families of the county — families Holloway, Bray, Wishart, Taylor, O'Keefe, Reynolds, and Quinney.

And more than these families, there were the families surrounding the farm, families including Kittleson, Dutcher, Johnson, Duesterbeck, Olson, Williams, Jacobson, Keltner, Larson, Nelson, Scola, and Gies. These were the families and farms of Sugar Creek Township that you will find on the plat map of the late 1800s and the years into the middle 1900s. The many rural schools and churches that dotted the map served to make a community. It takes a community to make a family farm.

Our farm of 160 acres was started as a few acres purchased in 1868 by our great-grandparents shortly after emigrating from Ireland. The farm, always a subsistence farm, survives after 144

years. Our father and mother reduced the amount of farming as they aged and as their sons left the farm to seek other lives. Our mother rented the acres for 30 years after our father died. We inherited the farm with her passing in 1999 at the age of 92. The farm survives intact, but it survives without the many things that once made it a family farm in a community of family farms.

The farm survives, for the time being, as land for a sustainable agriculture. A community-supported vegetable garden occupies a good portion of the farm. We have sought to improve the land and protect the woodlands and wetlands. Still, this is a transition to what we do not yet know. The land in the beginning was not for us to own. Might the land again become a common ground? A common ground for our time here on Earth.

Seven
We Shall Not Cease from Exploration

I<small>N THE</small> D<small>IAMOND</small> S<small>UTRA</small>, the Buddha looked within himself and found nothing fixed. Nothing separate, determinate, unchanging, no self distinguished from everything else. Only through grasping, holding on to views, do we try to halt the flow of things. Develop a mind that alights not upon anything. Thought is in itself an attempt to stop life. All beings and things are dependent on all other beings and things. We are constantly in flux, arising and dying in each moment. Change is the fundamental reality. Nothing remains the same. This fleeting world, a flickering lamp, a phantom, and a dream.

And yet I readily assume a separate self, an independence of things, and a world without change. I try heroically to preserve the family farm. Preservation of that which cannot be preserved in the flux of reality. Letting go, not being attached, would be the natural thing to do. Suffering the loss of what once existed is the price of continuing to hold on to what has no permanence. May I begin to practice the essence of the sutra. An absolute understanding is not readily apparent in this conditioned human world of ours.

As if seen while riding backward by the window of a fast-moving train, the land recedes as the train speeds forward. Time present recedes as another time is coming. Our view is of what has been. So little of the present moment we know.

I see my grandfather in the distance making his way across the field. He is in the seventy-eighth year of his life and I am nearly five. That would be the last year of my grandfather's life. I am now his age as he walked across the field toward me.

This is my first memory of anything in this world. All else recedes yearly in my mind, but this image remains clearly as if frozen in time. Without the farm where this took place, the true nature of my life would be diminished. Devoid of a separate identity, we all are an integral and indistinguishable part of everything. Without this awareness, we are homeless.

Lines of poetry for this time of my life. From T. S. Eliot's "Little Gidding" in his *Four Quartets*:

> We shall not cease from exploration
> And the end of all our exploring
> Will be to arrive where we started
> And know the place for the first time.

Pressing evermore is the desire to explore the wonder that I know as my life. Exploring where I came from, giving homage to the sources of my being, remembering the ancestors and all others who have come before me.

Eight
Out of Ireland

Descendants often speak my name, Bridget. Born Bridget O'Keefe in 1831 in Milltown, County Kilkenny. This is about all you know about me from the scant records of my life. The manifests of several ships during the 1840s list my name as a passenger. Some lists have me traveling with family and in others I am alone. You know from stories passed through the generations that I married John Quinney in 1850 while we were living in the Irish section of Yonkers, New York. No records have been found of our prior lives before fleeing the famine. Commoners, we were, anonymous, not subject to the keeping of records. Maybe someone, of a future generation, and still interested, will make the journey back to Ireland and learn more about who we were. We of the famine never returned.

What would have become of us if we had stayed in Ireland? Would we have survived the famine? Would we have been sent to the poor house? You might wonder how we gathered the funds to pay the passage to New York. How did John and I meet, and did we know each other before leaving County Kilkenny? What was our life like in the years in Yonkers before leaving for Wisconsin in 1859?

Our daughter Kate and son Tom were born in Yonkers. Over the waters and in wagons we made our way to the little community of Millard in Wisconsin, and for several years rented a couple of acres until we could make enough for down payment on the twenty acres a few miles south. This was 1868, and our family had grown with the birth of John and Bill and Mary. We lived in the house on the hill. My husband died much too young in 1880. Our son John farmed the land and added acres to the farm.

In 1895, I traveled by train to South Dakota to visit my sons Tom and Bill and their young families on the farms they homesteaded. They had immigrated to the Dakota Territory to claim homesteads in the 1880s. During my visit we all went to the photography studio of M. B. Barton in Alexandria to have our portrait made. I posed proudly between the families of Tom and Bill. You can now look into our eyes in that photograph and image our lives. We are saying to you that we too existed.

I became an old woman, and I passed away on a February day in 1920. Kate pasted in her scrapbook the brief obituary. Below the obituary she attached a poem.

> I did not weep.
> It seemed I did not know
> 'Twas endless sleep.
> And time went on —
> Drab days that groped or sped.
> Somehow I could not learn
> That she was dead.

I kept my faith to the end. Rosary in hand, I went to another place.

Bridget, mother of generations, you are a benchmark of my existence. In the realm of history, you are of the old world, and you came to the new world. Before you there were the ancestors from ancient times. In future historical time, there will be the descendants of us all. We of the present generation are in the midst of before and after. You and your ancestors exist in time present and time future. You, as with all of us, in birth and death, are beyond birth and death. The delusional dream is that of our birth and our death. The true reality, the ultimate reality, is no birth and no death.

Everything that has existed, and that exists now and will exist in the future, is interconnected and interdependent. In the words of the Prajnaparmita Sutra, all phenomena are marked by emptiness, neither produced nor destroyed, neither increasing nor decreasing. Nothing has a separate self, and nothing exists by itself. Everything is a part of everything else. Thich Nhat Hanh writes, "We are made of our mother and father, our grandmothers and grandfathers, our body, our feelings and our perceptions, our mental formations, the earth, the sun and innumerable non-self elements." Everything, including that which we know as ourselves, is in a constant state of creation. Understanding this, making this an integral part of our being, is to become enlightened about our true nature.

Walk by the old place where our ancestors made their home long ago. Among the lilac bushes and the remaining foundation of the old house, you will sense a presence that does not diminish with the years. You will know that you are a part of all that has ever existed. And when your heart and mind are ready, you will know that there is no birth and no death. There will be a peace, a release from the fear and anxiety of this relative existence.

Nine
A Handful of Things I Know

A LIFETIME and beyond of being John Quinney. I was born in 1860 in a rented house near Millard shortly before Mother and Father purchased the few acres that would become the farm. I lived in the house on the hill surrounded by lilacs with an orchard that sloped to the edge of the pond. I grew up there and never strayed far from the old place. I farmed the land, and tamed and worked horses for field and plow all of my life. My two brothers, Tom and Bill, went west in the eighties to claim homesteads. Sister Kate worked much of her life in Chicago as a seamstress and milliner. Mary married Henry Reynolds and raised a family a few miles away. My dear wife, Hattie, died much too young after the birth of our three children. I never married again, and I told anyone who asked that I would never find a wife as good as Hattie. Hattie, my dear Hattie.

Our Marjorie was born in 1895 a year after we were married. Floyd and Nellie were born at the beginning of the new century. After Hattie died in 1905, I did the best I could raising the children with the help of Mother and Kate. The years went by so fast. One of my last memories is from the final year of my life, 1939, and I am walking, troubled by arthritis, across the field to the farm buildings. Floyd and his sons are watching as I slowly make my way toward them. My grandson will for the rest of his life remember this as being his first memory, and the only time he remembers ever seeing me.

There are very few living now that remember hearing anything about me. Hardly anyone remains who actually saw me. A neighbor's granddaughter recently told someone that her grandfather and I visited often and worked together with our horses. Little remains of tangible evidence that I ever existed. There is the fading photograph from Marjorie's album of me standing behind the grain drill, with the team of horses, in the field near the old house. Standing tall with mustache, squinting into the light. This is the picture that my descendants will show of me as their ancestor. A leather harness, a feedbag, a horse collar, and a cap still hang on the dusty wall of the granary. An iron horseshoe dug up from the field has been nailed to the side of the chicken house east of the barn.

Generations later it is said that I was the best breaker and tamer of horses in the county. I've heard it said that I could "break a horse with one arm," but what that means I don't know. I do admit that I was rightly recognized as being good with horses. Many of the horses were the mustangs rounded up wild in the West, shipped to Clinton, Iowa, and bought by farmers in Iowa, Illinois, and Wisconsin. I worked hard farming the land, milking the cows, and taming the horses. I can't recall the times I did much more than work on the farm.

You could say that horses were in my blood. Blood carried in the veins of my mother and father when they came from Ireland during the famine. My dreams at night were of wild horses running

in the moonlight. As I worked the fields by day, horses in harnesses made my living. You can imagine me now running and working and resting with horses. A rider in the sky, you might imagine.

Did I dance with another after Hattie passed away? Did I go to town on Saturday nights? Did I drink beer at the tavern in Millard? Behind my back neighbors would tell their friends, "He is a man of few words." When I talked I had a bit of the accent of the Irish, learned from my parents. But I tried hard to fit into the ways of my emigrant neighbors from Norway, Germany, England, and Bohemia. We all knew we were foreign to this country, and we wanted to be accepted and not noticed as being different.

You'll find little evidence that I put pen to paper for reasons other than the occasional legal document. Two or three years before we were married, I wrote a few words with my own hand in Hattie's little red autograph book. On February 6, 1891, I wrote in a fair, slanting script these lines to Hattie:

> I don't go much on religion
> I never aint had no Show
> But I got a middlin tight grip Sir
> On the handful of things I know.

I signed as *J. Quinney, Delavan.* A practical man, as you can see, with a proper wooing for a wife I had in mind even then.

Hattie and I were married in the Methodist Church. Sister Kate remained a Catholic all her life. Brother Bill and his family followed the Catholic religion in South Dakota. Mary became a Methodist and passed her faith through the generations of her family. I wasn't much for church services on Sunday mornings, with chores my calling. Mother was always a Catholic of the old country. She attended Sunday morning mass at Saint Andrew's Church, as long she was able. In the early years she walked the five miles to the church in Delavan each Sunday morning. She had a religious faith to carry her the forty years after my father died in 1880. Father had a bit of the superstition from the old country, sometimes telling us about the little creatures that inhabited thickets, marsh, and woodlands.

Hattie's folks were of a long line of devout Christians. Her ancestors came from England as Puritans and settled in the colonies. Her father, Nathan Church Reynolds, with the long gray beard of a prophet from the Old Testament, descended from a Salem family accused of witchcraft. His ancestors fought in the American Revolution.

The siblings of Hattie made for a large family. Her brother Seymour lived with us until the night he slipped on a patch of snow-covered ice while carrying a log back to the house to keep the fire burning throughout the cold night. We found him three days later covered in snow with his dog waiting beside him. Hattie and I kept in contact with her five sisters who led their own tragic lives, some dying young of consumption, as did Hattie.

Hattie looks out at us with our baby in a portrait made in Delavan the year of Marjorie's birth. There is also the portrait of the six sisters, beautifully dressed, standing beside each other, with Hattie in the back row. And there is the large oval portrait of Hattie before our marriage. My son's wife wrote on the back of the portrait, for posterity, "Floyd's Mother." And there is the picture of me years later, in one of the albums, standing with neighbors in a farmyard.

Eleven years of marriage we had. Fortunate were the children and I to have had the help of Kate and Mother after Hattie left us. Throughout the years, the lamps flickered during the winter evenings in the dark rooms of the house on the hill. Kate, finally living in the house alone, survived me by a couple of years. She placed into her album the brief obituary, my death notice, from the newspaper in town.

Ten
As Long as We Are Remembered

MY DAUGHTER, ALICE, kept a framed photograph of me on the table beside her chair the last years of her life. I left her when she was but a child. Bright's disease took me from family and friends in the prime of my life at the age of thirty-eight in 1921. We had just moved from the farm up the road to our new house in Millard. My husband, Will Holloway, and Alice had to adjust to a life without wife and mother. I, Lorena, remained in the memories of my daughter and her children. As memories fade and descendants pass, I too may join the generations no longer remembered.

In my thirty-eight years, I lived with the stories that were told of ancestors in the few generations before me. My mother told us about her parents, James and Joyce Wishart, deceased by the time I was born. Her father had made a living as the blacksmith in La Grange. He emigrated from England in 1828, settled for a few years in Clinton, New York, and came to Wisconsin in 1844. His father and mother, John and Ann, emigrated with him and lived the last years in La Grange. According to the account in *La Grange Pioneers,* John was a sturdy Scot, a mason by trade, a great reader and intelligent talker, pious in character and temperate in his habits of life. Ann, with maiden name of Stockdale, is described as a woman of deep piety and noble character and like her husband was of Scottish birth and parentage. James and Joyce had ten children, and my mother, Ellen, always called Nellie, was the last-born of the children.

My mother married Charles Taylor, and they farmed and lived in the large Greek Revival house beside the road in La Grange. You may have seen the photograph of our family posing on the front lawn of our house. Little is remembered and hardly anything is told about my childhood. I know that an old newspaper clipping and a few artifacts have been found to document the family tragedy of the loss of my sister, Leah, in her youth. In one of the family trunks was found a six-by-ten-inch black cardboard box with *Writing Desk* spelled out in embossed letters that had belonged to my sister. A few of Leah's belongings were placed in it when she died at the age of ten in 1888: penciled lists of school grades, colored cards of dancing children, a small roll of mending materials with thread, needle, and pins. There is an ornate metal plate engraved *Leah — Our Darling*. And the obituary from the local newspaper.

A long time ago we children carried flowers and placed them upon the grave of my sister. My brother Leo died a year later at the age of two, and the procession again went to the cemetery on the hill. My brother Lloyd and I remained with Mother and Father to grow up on the farm

Will Holloway, who lived on the neighboring farm, and I married on a February day in 1903. Alice, our one and only, was born in 1906. Will recorded the birth along with other notes about preparing the land for spring planting. Our family of three went about our daily chores in tune with the seasons. We visited regularly and gathered for celebrations with relatives that lived close by. Alice would become the recorder of our lives in the diary that she kept and in the many photographs she took with her camera. Beginning in January of 1916, when she was nine years old, she wrote faithfully each day for five years until the end of 1920. What you know of our family, and of me during my last years, can be gleaned from Alice's childhood diary. You can read a few entries to know something about our time together.

Papa went to church and mama and I stayed home. It was 20 below zero. (January 7, 1916)

I took my camera to school. Teacher showed me how to take a picture. Teacher took a picture of me. Jack (my cat) would not hold still so I could not take his picture. We went to Millard and back in the car. I wore my hat to school. (May 4, 1916)

We had a short auto ride. Took Grandma's picture. I had the headache all day. Papa and I went to the woods. I took a picture of mama and papa in the car. Papa took a picture of me at night. (May 7, 1916)

Did not go to school. I was not sick. I was lazy. Papa painted some of the garage. Jack (is my cat) slept with me in the afternoon. I got up at 4:30 p.m. Papa painted the milk house. (May 8, 1916)

Went to Delavan. Got mama's coat and mine. From Delavan went to Aunt Lizzie's. (March 28, 1917)

Went to Janesville. Pa bought a hog. Ma a new dress. Then went to Whitewater and got a pair of grey topped shoes. Bought Uncle Lloyd a sugar spoon & butter knife. At night went to Palmyra. (September 29, 1917)

Ma got up early and washed. I was making ma a Xmas present at school. Pa finished tax roll. (December 17, 1917)

It was Christmas. Went up to Grandma's. Uncle Lloyd and Elsie were there. Had more presents. Got a gold thimble. (December 25, 1917)

Everyone got out and broke roads. No school. Beautiful day. Snow 4 feet deep in the road. Uncle Lloyd put cattle in the new barn. (January 14, 1918)

We went to Delavan to the picnic in Tilden's woods. A soldier that had been a prisoner in Germany 2 years spoke. (August 28, 1918)

Had salt fish for dinner. (Drank water all the afternoon.) Mama and I picked ducks. Feathers all over. (October 24, 1918)

Went to school. Telegram came saying Germany had surrendered. We rang the school bell. The church bells rang in the towns. They rang for an hour. Everyone was excited. (November 7, 1918)

The report was not so. That the war was over. Went to school. (November 8, 1918)

Report came that the war was over. (It is so this time.) Got word at 2 o'clock a.m. People celebrated all day. Went to Elkhorn at night. (November 11, 1918)

Grandma and Grandpa came down to dinner. We had duck and ice cream. Was a little colder at night. I have had a cough all day. (January 1, 1919)

Was my birthday. Got a pair of silk gloves and silk stockings from mama and a box of candy from papa. (April 29, 1919)

Ma and pa went to Janesville after a pony. Bought Trixy. Ma drove her home. Trixy is 4 years old. (July 25, 1919)

Went to school. Grandma died in the morning. Rained. (September 30, 1919)

Cold. We did not go to church. Grandpa came down to supper. November has been cold with lots of rain. Up to now I have driven to school every day and put Trixy in Patchen's barn. (November 30, 1919)

We and Uncle Lloyd and Aunt Elsie and Grandpa went to Uncle Frank's to dinner. Snowed and drifted the night before. 18 below. We were going sleigh riding at night, but it was too cold. (January 1, 1920)

School picnic at Turtle Lake. Got my diploma and standings. Was valedictorian of my class. (June 4, 1920)

Rained. Papa went to town with oats. An aeroplane went over. (June 17, 1920)

Fine day. We all went to Racine. Aunt Rachel went with us. In the afternoon went to the shore of Lake Michigan. At night went to a vaudeville. (August 7, 1920)

Went up to Uncle Lloyd's. Mrs. Uglow and Myrtle and Elva were there. Had a swell dinner. Stayed to supper. Had oysters. (December 25, 1920)

Alice stopped writing in her diary shortly after I passed away. In 1930 she married Floyd Quinney. They farmed together and raised two sons. Floyd died tending chores in 1969, and Alice remained on the farm into her ninety-second year. My dear daughter Alice was the keeper of our lives.

A few strands of my hair were saved in a little round box. My tattered and well-used book of hymns to save the soul survived and occasionally comes into the light of day. The hymn I pasted inside the front cover waits for another voice. I had faith that there was more to this life than what appeared. And my consolation: "When all my labors and trials are o'er, and I am safe on that beautiful shore." Oh, that will be glory for me.

Eleven
A Spiritual Life

THE VENERABLE SUBHUTI thanks the Buddha for being the example for daily living and asks how he and other disciples might attain liberation. The Diamond Sutra ends with a summation of the teaching of wisdom and compassion, a wisdom and a compassion that are attained without grasping, explained without explaining. The Buddha gets up each morning and goes to town. Buddhahood, which we have never been without, is like a diamond that cuts through illusion.

You came to your senses — to your consciousness — as you watched your grandfather coming toward you across the field from the old place. Soon after you would find yourself lying on your back in the grass in the same field looking into the blue sky with the floating white clouds and seeing the face of the founding father of your country. You knew instantly, then, that you had been chosen, called to a life of significant meaning. That your life would be spiritual as much as it would be material. Your life from then on would be marked and measured by events with the spiritual and material intimately joined. Bringing you to where you are now.

You inherited deep and steady religious traditions from generations of ancestors. Your maternal ancestors were Reformation

Protestants who emigrated from the midlands of England during the first half of the nineteenth century. They carried with them the King James scriptures contained in the well-worn family bibles. They built Methodist churches wherever they lived as they moved westward to Wisconsin. They attended services regularly and faithfully for the rest of their lives. Daily life on the farm was grounded in a religious community of fellow believers. The cemeteries in La Grange and Sugar Creek townships contain the remains of the ancestors that gave you body and spirit.

Your father's ancestors practiced the Catholic religion for generations before the emigration from famine Ireland. You can only speculate about the practice of religion in earlier and ancient times. Some ancestors likely carried the genetic and psychic makeup of the Celts, the Vikings, the Anglo-Saxons, and the stone-age tribes of earlier migrations across Europe. Worship could have been in the forests among the trees. Each time you walked down to the old place — the home of the three generations that preceded you — you sensed spirits inhabiting the remains of the old house, and sensed a presence among the oaks and maples and willows surrounding the old place. Crows in the high branches watched as you walked through the tall grass. Red-winged blackbirds sang to the coming of spring, and great blue herons flew into the tamaracks in the marsh.

The black rosaries of your great-grandmother and great-aunt rested on the dusty attic floor of the farmhouse all the years of your childhood. Each night at bedtime you said your prayer. "Now

I lay me down to sleep." You prayed the Lord your soul to keep. On Sundays you learned the stories from the Bible and sang in the church choir. On Easter Sunday morning you gathered at the lake with fellow worshippers and watched once again the signs of resurrection. Not that you certainly believed the beliefs, but you knew that something, something mysterious beyond knowing, was being observed. You knew that as you aged you would always be of the spiritual world.

The first big move of your life began as you were driven, a distance of thirty-five miles, by your parents to the college you would attend for the next four years. You were being taken from the land and home of your first eighteen years of life. True, you were somewhat prepared by the years of high school in town. It had taken the freshman and sophomore years in Delavan High School to adjust to the ways and expectations of townspeople. There had been the appendectomy you insisted upon to relieve the anxiety and pains suffered each morning on the way to school. Some sense of well-being came with participation in school activities, the making of friends, and courses and classes. You learned to play the trombone, eventually fronting a dance band and playing "Star Dust" as fellow students danced into the night on the gymnasium floor. All of this was well beyond the eight years in the one-room school in the country. In later years you knew that the rural school and the life of farming gave you a foundation for all that would follow.

Missed most of all during the first year of college, especially at bedtime, were the voices of your father and mother. And you missed gathering around the kitchen table in the farmhouse for breakfast, dinner, and supper. You experienced the loneliness of being away from home. All the homes you have made in the course of a life have echoed the one known at the farm. You could never leave home for long.

Your achievements in college were a way to adapt to a world beyond the farm. Being elected president of the student body seemed to be an indication of acceptance by others. You dated and danced, and joined a fraternity to be able to live in a house at the edge of the campus. The summer between the junior and senior years you drove with a group of students from the Wesley Fellowship to a revival meeting at Lake Poinsett, South Dakota. At the end of the week, gathered around a campfire at night, you all were asked to come forward one by one to seek salvation. You were the only one who did not go forward. A spiritual life for you would have to be personal and practiced from within. Graduation from college took place in 1956 on a beautiful Sunday afternoon. Family and relatives surrounded you.

What were you to do with your life? You remember the listening and the waiting to be *called*. The question would persist throughout your life, but now was the time to make immediate decisions. You had majored in biology and psychology and sociology, and you had thought about pursuing a career in one of the medical professions. The summer spent working in the credit office of a Chicago hospital turned you away from a possible career in hospital administration. An earlier summer of working as an orthopedic orderly in a hospital made you certain that you did not want to be a doctor. And unrelated, but always a thought, was to be a minister, a Methodist minister like those you had known and admired for their calling while you were growing up.

Late in the summer, as medical professions faded in your mind, you were drawn to the questions posed in your undergraduate sociology courses. And you thought about the many teachers who had been important in your education. On impulse, but surely more than that, you removed your car from storage and drove up Lake Shore Drive along Lake Michigan to the campus of Northwestern University. You met with Kimball Young, the head of the Sociology Department, in his apartment in Evanston. He welcomed you to the fold, and he would be your advisor, and you would be his research and teaching assistant for the year. The grandson of Brigham Young was pointing the way for a life that could be of service to others.

The next twenty years your spiritual life was away from theistic religion, beyond a God-centered spirituality. Graduate school presented questions that could be answered adequately in secular terms. You were told, in fact, to give up spiritual concerns in the pursuit of science. A world without God was world enough, and most likely the real one. You were well on the way to being an existentialist as well as a scientist. You would regard this as your spiritual life. A spiritual life that was grounded in daily life and in the family that you were now creating.

You became politically aware during the 1960s while living and teaching in New York City. Academic work was informed by your involvement in the civil rights and antiwar movements. You immersed yourself in the popular culture of the times. Walking the streets of the city, camera in hand, you observed a world intensely. You began to write each day, and your writing became part of your spiritual life, part of your calling.

Then came the time, as the sixties ended and the seventies began, to leave the city. Consumption, both material and cultural, began to overwhelm mind and spirit. In need of a quieter life, a more meditative life, you took a leave from university teaching and moved with your family to North Carolina for three years. There would be explorations of many kinds. You traveled and gave lectures. You wrote books. You often visited your mother on the farm, and you missed your father who had passed away on a November day in 1969.

Providence, the city and the inspiration, would be a home for the next ten years. These would be the years of an explicit return to matters of the spirit. One day your daughter asked for involvement in a religious community. This led to attendance at the First Baptist Church in America, the church founded by Roger Williams, with a minister well grounded in the neo-orthodox theology of Tillich, Niebuhr, and Bonhoeffer. Eventually you and your family would attend the services and activities of the First Unitarian

Church of Providence. It was there that you began the Buddhist studies and practices that would become the basis of your spiritual life. You found what you had never lost.

A return to the Midwest, your true home, was necessary and inevitable. You were now within sixty miles of the farm, teaching sociology at Northern Illinois University. You regularly visited your mother at the farm, photographed the landscape of the county, wrote daily in the journals that would become books, created friendships, and lived close to the rhythms of a deliberate life. Your younger daughter left home for college, and you became a grandfather when your older daughter gave birth. There would be a crisis and change in your household with divorce and a new marriage.

You were aging and you became ill with chronic leukemia. At the turn of the century, after you retired from teaching, you and your wife moved to Madison, finally returning to Wisconsin forty years after leaving in the summer of 1960. You found ways to preserve the family farm after your mother passed away as the new century was about to begin. There seemed to be a rounding to your life.

Others have told you that you have lived a spiritual life. From your perspective, your life has been a constant and perpetual search for meaning. You have thought of yourself as a pilgrim. Several religious traditions have been studied and integrated into your sense of who are and how you should live. You have tried to live a good life, a life that is of service to others, a life that follows the perennial guidance of the Golden Rule of doing unto others as you would have others do unto you.

Here in the winter of your life, you struggle to maintain a faith in the wonder of existence. You seek to be fully alive in the course of aging with its pains and increasing infirmities. Engagement and optimism are part of the work of a continuing spiritual life. You greet the day with a faith in life, and you are aware that the meaning of existence is ultimately unknowable. Absolute reality will always remain a mystery. The distinction between life and death is a construct of the human mind. Your life began long before your birth. Going on in the face of the mystery is the life of the pilgrim. The journey is the essence of the spiritual life.

Twelve
The Visual World

IT IS NOVEMBER. This is how I am living my life. This is what I am doing with my life. The ephemeral world as we know it is marked by the daily news. Barack Obama has been elected to a second term as President. Millions of people on the East Coast are recovering from Hurricane Sandy. The FBI discovered letters that reveal an affair by the CIA director. The wars continue in Syria and Afghanistan. An early play by Chekhov is being staged in New York. The latest James Bond movie is on screens across the nation. The poor remain poor and the rich get richer as new tax proposals are debated.

A bright sun shines through the window on this crisp autumn morning. This is clearly evident to the human eye. For centuries, the teaching of the sutra has held the vision of a diamond blade cutting through worldly illusions to reveal what is real and everlasting. Do you sometimes see through the illusions of this world? Is such clarity possible? For the time being, perhaps for all time, kindness with a compassionate heart is reality enough.

And in these times when words are few and thoughts are far between, what fills your conscious life? You dream your days away. With intention to live deliberately, as Henry David Thoreau advised, you turn to what has sustained you all your life — beyond

words and thoughts. You turn to a world of visual delight. Seeing, composing a world in a viewfinder, is your work and solace. With camera in hand, this bright autumn day, you go to the children's park a few blocks from your house, to the park designed years ago by the landscape architect Jens Jensen. For the moment, this is all that needs to be done in your world of dreams. Photographs of bedrock below and trees soaring into the sky. Grounded and vanishing all at once.

Thirteen
The Written Word

Darkness was coming to the Illinois prairie. And we were three hours from home and tired after driving all day from Memphis. The exit sign on Interstate 55 pointed to the town of Lincoln. The road took us several miles along a stretch of old Route 66 on the outskirts of town, and then back to the Interstate. I had wanted to see, however brief the time would be, the hometown of writer William Maxwell. Decades ago I had read his book *So Long, See You Tomorrow*. Without that book, it is likely that I would not be sitting at this table writing these lines about my world of dreams.

   Maxwell and his biographer, Barbara Burkhardt, met for days over the years to gather material about his life as a writer. In his New York apartment and at his country house north of the city, she would ask him a question and he would place a sheet of paper into his typewriter and carefully compose his answer. He could think on the typewriter better than talking, he told her. There are writers who speak eloquently in interviews. There are other writers who compose and convey their thoughts, their creations, best in writing. Is not writing, for many, the only feasible way of expressing thoughts and ideas, characters and plots and stories? In the writing, only in the writing, worlds are brought forth, worlds that might not exist without the imagination and the writing of the words. Words that come from the writer's need to write. A writer's secret knowledge: I write, therefore I am.

Composing and typing his answers, Maxwell said this about his writing: "I have a melancholy feeling that all human experience goes down the drain, or to put it politely, ends in oblivion, except when somebody records some part of his own experience — which can of course be the life that goes on in his mind and imagination as well as what he had for breakfast." Autobiographical fiction over the course of Maxwell's life, in a succession of novels and stories, has given some degree of permanence to the lives of people he knew and loved. We, the readers, have a record of how this writer thought and what he experienced over the course of his life from childhood to old age. Past and present always meet in his writing, as Maxwell's biographer notes, stretching before him like the land and sky of his midwestern landscape.

We returned to the highway, saving an extended visit to Lincoln and the sites of Maxwell's early years for another time. We turned north in the dark night and made our way home. Silently giving thanks for a visit with family now spread across this land of pioneers.

Here in our town, in an apartment near the center of town, was born in 1897 the child that would become the writer Thornton Wilder. In the play *Our Town,* which he wrote in the mid-1930s, he has the young Emily, who has returned to earth for one day, ask, "Do any human beings ever realize life while they live it? — every, every minute?" The Stage Manager is guiding the audience through the town of the now departed. Primal questions are being explored: How do we live? How do we survive? What is love and how does it help with the difficulties of living, of being good? Income from the play and the earlier novel *The Bridge of San Luis Rey* helped to support the large Wilder family of parents and often struggling siblings. In the novel, the Abbess says in the memorable conclusion, "There is a land of the living and a land of the dead and the bridge is love, the only survival, the only meaning." But the existentialist and ever-questioning Wilder, years later in the play *The Alcestiad*, has Alcestis say, "Yes, but love is not enough. Love is not the meaning. It is one of the signs that there is a meaning." Somewhere in the living of daily life, the universal — and the eternal — is to be found. Later in his life, in the solitude of a desert, writing the novel *The Eighth Day,* Wilder found some consolation in the idea that we as part of nature are ever evolving. Creation has not ended.

In all his writing, Wilder struggled with the question of how to live one's life. He searched for an answer, reconciliation, in his living and his writing, in the evolution of both the living and the writing. Always the central question: "How do we live, knowing that we will die?"

Four days before Wilder died, his biographer tells us, he wrote friends, "I am now old, really old, and these recent set-backs have taken a lot of energy out of me." Not giving up, still with the hope of further writing, he wrote, "I think I'm pulling myself together for another piece of work."

Jupiter appears in the night sky. And around it the constellation Orion, the Pleiades, and the bright star Hyades. A long time ago, three magi on camels crossed a desert leading to the town of Bethlehem of Judea. There had been foretelling of something miraculous about to happen. The Gospel of Matthew later would tell that the magi found mother and child and made offerings from treasure chests. Christian traditions would celebrate the Epiphany, the revelation that the son of God has come to earth. With a crucifixion and a resurrection, the religion of the incarnated Jesus Christ was founded.

In the poem "Journey of the Magi" by T. S. Eliot, one of the magi describes their journey and arrival "not a moment too soon" for the birth of Jesus. "A hard time we had of it," he says, with the thought that possibly it all was folly. Each year I listen to Eliot's recording of the poem, and I gaze at the painting by James Tissot of the three magi making their way out of the mountains and into the desert. Eliot, as he writes his poem, has converted to the Anglican Church, and the old ways, for him and the magi, are fading.

He, who was born in the manger, eventually, will be placed on a cross to die. The new religion will hold the promise of resurrection and everlasting life. Christmas is of the birth; the rest of the story will come later. This time of year prompts a questioning of the old dispensations, and we too are far from ease. This is life's challenge and adventure as we join the caravan crossing the desert each year as winter comes.

Fourteen
Transcendent Dreams

Who is this dreamer? I am recording the dreams that come to me. I am recording the life I am living. Where do these dreams come from that I bring to you? Surely, the dreams that I dream are of a much larger, collective dream. We do not dream alone.

This is what I see today through the tall windows of my living room. The light of the morning sky dances across the night's freshly fallen snow. Branches of pine, spruce, and birch glisten. Three squirrels jump from the limb of the locust onto the balcony and find seeds fallen from the feeder. I watch as cardinals, chickadees, and sparrows feast. The snowplow will not come to our street for another day. I was born to love the winter.

My dreams are firmly grounded in a world of transcendence. Within my being, as they must be, but founded on all that is outside of me. I am part and parcel of the universe and perhaps a cosmos beyond the universe. I am not the first to know that I contain multitudes. That I have no separate existence, that I am everything.

And often I imagine myself as a Henry David Thoreau wintering in a cabin in the woods at Walden Pond. I am part of the long tradition of the transcendentalists. My dreaming life comes out of the philosophies of English romantic poetry, German idealism, Eastern religions, and the practical wisdom of all people seeking and living a deliberate life daily. An inner truth founded on personal intuition transcends the dreamer. No better apprehended than in a yearly reading of the writings of Thoreau.

My life's calling, shared with Thoreau, has been that of actively observing the world. At the beginning of his account of going to live in the woods beside Walden Pond, he wrote, "For many years I was self-appointed inspector of snow storms and rain storms, and did my duty faithfully." Thoreau found a universe within himself and in the landscape close to home. He was fully employed in the daily observations and reflections that he noted in his daily writing.

This winter I think especially about Thoreau's visit to the Midwest near the end of his life. I think of him sitting in the coach car looking out the window far from his New England home. For years Thoreau had suffered the effects of tuberculosis. Finally in 1861, the year before he died, his doctor advised him to seek a change of climate. The doctor suggested that he take a long journey to the West Indies or the South of France or the Mississippi Valley. Perhaps because of the lower cost of a trip to the Midwest or because of his interest in American flora and fauna, Thoreau decided to travel to Minnesota. The journey began from Concord, Massachusetts, on the eleventh of May and ended when he returned home on the tenth of July.

After stopping at Niagara Falls and Detroit for a few days, Thoreau and his traveling companion, Horace Mann Jr., a student of botany, reached Chicago on May 21. Resting for a couple of days at the Metropolitan House, visiting a Unitarian minister, they bought tickets for the train trip to Saint Paul, Minnesota. Thoreau saw the prairie for the first time as the train rolled across northern Illinois to Dunleith. From the port on the Mississippi, Thoreau and Mann went up the river by boat, stopping along the way at Prairie du Chien, Wisconsin. From their room in Saint Paul, Mann wrote a letter to his mother, saying that Mr. Thoreau "is doing very well now and I think will be a great deal better before long."

Thoreau's journal of the trip is devoted mainly to natural history. He went to geological and botanical museums, talked to naturalists, read books and reports, gathered and identified many specimens, and searched eagerly for a wild crab apple tree. He observed and noted the many species of birds and animals — wild pigeons in enormous flocks, turkey buzzards and herons, kingfishers and jays, swallows, ducks, and turtles. He showed little interest in frontier life and was embarrassed by a Sioux Indian dance staged in Redwood for the party of travelers.

At the end of June, Thoreau was ready to return home. He and Mann left Minnesota on the twenty-sixth for Prairie du Chien. They then took the train to Milwaukee, passing through Madison at one thirty in the afternoon. They reached Concord the second week of July, traveling by way of Mackinaw City, Toronto, Ogdensburg, Vermont, and New Hampshire. I think now of Thoreau, on the train, passing within a few blocks of my house.

The excursion totaled thirty-five hundred miles, the longest trip Thoreau had ever made. Even at that, Thoreau had cut the trip short by a month or more, possibly because of homesickness and certainly because of the continuing illness in his chest. Some years ago, a literary commentator, John T. Flanagan, suggested a reason for Thoreau's early return: "Possibly also he realized that there was no cure for him, and he desired to spend his final lingering days in the setting endeared to him by nature and man. In any event, he never left home again." Becoming weaker during the winter, Thoreau died on May 6, 1862.

Near the end, a friend had asked Thoreau how the opposite shore appeared to him. Thoreau answered, summing up the way he had lived his whole life, "One world at a time." In a last letter, Thoreau observed the effects of the night's rain on the gravel of the railroad causeway. Thoreau concluded the letter: "All this is perfectly distinct to an observant eye, and yet could easily pass unnoticed by most. Thus each wind is self-registering." Earlier he had noted that each life is self-registering. We make our observations, take a few notes, and pass on.

Fifteen
Lovely, Dark, and Deep

THE RIDER IN THE SLEIGH stops his horse to watch the woods fill up with snow. This is a strange thing to be doing.

> My little horse must think it queer
> To stop without a farmhouse near
> Between the woods and frozen lake
> The darkest evening of the year.

For the rider in the sleigh, pausing for a time, "the woods are lovely, dark and deep." He moves on with the life that must be lived.

I sit at the table on my bench that might as well be the seat of a sleigh passing in the woods on a snowy evening. My few words — a mix of reverie and meditation — are offered before I resume the daily chores. These times of sitting at the table are lovely, dark, and deep. As if stopping in the woods on a snowy evening.

And there are promises to keep. The Diamond Sutra to contemplate. This photograph to show you of a horse and sleigh in front of a house near my mother's childhood farm. It may be that she took the photograph with her camera. Or possibly she is the rider in the sleigh. A long time ago, nearly a hundred years, and the house still

stands. I will keep a copy of this photograph on the table beside my chair throughout the winter.

The Buddha is trying to help Subhuti unlearn preconceived notions of reality. Instructing that all thoughts of reality are illusory, that thoughts cannot grasp reality and must be set aside if enlightenment is to be found. Are we always, then, seeing through a glass darkly as we attempt to perceive what is happening? In the Diamond Sutra we, as devotees, are urged to cut through the illusions of reality. Understanding that thoughts, both concrete and abstract, are mental constructs that mask the true reality underlying them. How can we cut through thoughts and find the true reality? To find the unconditioned reality that knows no change, decay, or death? Beyond impermanence, is there a fixed essence, a truth beyond our human imagination?

For us, humans in the flux of our lives, the Buddha offers "the middle way." We can give our attention to daily meditation and to lives of compassion. A middle way between illusion and complete enlightenment. It is enlightenment enough to be practicing right action and the seeking of understanding. This is the life of a pilgrim on a spiritual journey.

We humans may never see clearly. Knowing ultimate reality is beyond our human capacity. But what is left is our responsibility to create and apply constructs of thought that make us compassionate and lead us to acts of kindness. We are active participants in the thoughts we think and in the lives we lead in relation to these thoughts. We are constantly borrowing the constructions all around us. My writings are filled with literary references, with the creative constructions of others. I choose to use the constructions that come to me in the course of my daily life.

The true nature of reality can never be known by us, certainly not in our current state of evolution as a species. But through our meditation and practices we can be aware of our conditioned existence, of our human condition. And realizing our conditioned existence, and the impermanence of this existence, we live our lives with care for one another and for ourselves. We recognize that we do not have a fixed identity, no separate self, and that we are a part of everything. That is world enough.

Sixteen
Our Days and Nights Together

We married, on a beautiful summer's day in 1924. It was Will's fifty-second year and my forty-second. For nearly twenty years I had taught in the county schools. When Will Holloway and I, Mabel Stiles, married, three years had passed since the death of his wife, Lorena. He and their daughter, Alice, had continued to live in the newly built house next to the Millard store at the corner of Highways A and O. Alice had graduated from Elkhorn High School and was about to begin the rural education program at the State Normal School in Whitewater when we married that summer. This would be our home for the rest of our lives. Alice, after teaching school for five years, married Floyd Quinney and settled into a life in the farmhouse three miles from us.

I grew up in Whitewater as one of the three sisters in the Stiles family. Lenore married Julius Johnson and lived in the large house on the corner, across from the Millard store, a short walk from our house. Myrtle and her husband, Henry Miller, lived only a few miles away in Fort Atkinson. We visited each other several times a week for the rest of our lives.

Look at the many photographs in our family album and sort through the photos gathered from the drawers of chests and desks and you will know more about the life that Will and I had together for thirty-five years. You will see our garden in the summer, parties on the front lawn, snow piled high in the driveway, our evenings around the dinner table, holiday gatherings, snapshots of our trips throughout the state, and our days at the annual county fair.

I kept a diary for the year 1939. It survives, being rescued from a desk drawer as Alice's farmhouse was being cleared for the last time seventy years later. You will notice the large hole that a mouse nibbled in the spine of the diary. Enough remains for you to know about the way Will and I lived our lives together.

At diary's end, I wrote that we were ready to turn our faces toward the dawn of a new year. Looking back I am amazed at all that we did in the course of a year. We were busy, always on the move, working and playing, visiting family and friends, attending meetings and ceremonies, baking and canning, caring for our health, and seeing the sights. Life is the accumulation of all we have done in the course of our days and nights together.

On a Sunday, as the year began, Will made ice cream. We cooked a dinner for the aunts — chicken, dressing, and squash. I made cookies and Jell-O with whipped cream. We were invited to Millers, and stopped at the aunts with the dinner, setting the table for them, and had them eating when we left. We spent a pleasant day at the Millers, and had roast goose and all the trimmings. We took ice cream and cake. We stopped at the aunts on our way home. Julia had our dishes all washed. We reached home at nine, just in time to hear J. Anthony on the radio. Madison folks were at Johnsons. A beautiful day and evening.

The next day we were invited to go with the Wiswells to the inauguration in Madison. We left before nine. There were about ten thousand people at the Capitol. We had a hard time getting located but finally found a good place on the stairs. We could see and hear about everything. We made reservations at the Park Hotel and left after the inauguration for a fine perch dinner at the hotel. Then Wyman drove us all to the governor's mansion so we had a passing glimpse of it. We reached home at four, and went over to Johnsons in the evening. Spent a very pleasant day.

During the second week of March we attended the golden wedding celebration at Millard Hall for Mr. and Mrs. Alfred Pollard. I helped with decorating and also helped to clean up. Alice and the boys came and invited us over for supper on Saturday evening in honor of Floyd's birthday. I was sick for a day, sleeping in the afternoon. The next morning Will went to Delavan for a tractor show. In the evening we made ice cream and went over to Quinneys. We had a fine meal for Floyd's birthday and stayed until nearly ten. The next day, Sunday, we went to church in Delavan and had dinner in town.

On a day near the end of March, I cleaned the kitchen cupboard. Julius came over for dinner. We had corn beef and cabbage and cherry pie. In the afternoon, I washed the kitchen windows and cleaned the floors in the kitchen and the front porch. Made a pie for Browns and took it over. I then took a walk in Johnsons' orchard. It was so warm I had to take off my coat and cap. Will went up to the farm in the morning, and in the afternoon he went down to Willard's to balance books. Mother is still papering at her farm. Julius went over this afternoon to paint.

On Good Friday, Will and I went to church at Elkhorn with Lenore, Mother, and Jean. It snowed terribly coming home. Lenore had to stop several times and get out to wipe the windshield. On Saturday I had my hair set. On Easter Sunday we went to Delavan to church. Wore my new hat, blue dress, and coat. We drove to Fort Atkinson for dinner.

Where does the time go? Summer will be ending soon. This week I canned twenty-four quarts of tomato juice and twenty-five pints of applesauce. I have made two batches of crab apple jelly. The European war started. I hope we will keep out of it. England and France are going to help the Poles against the Germans. We did not go to the fair as Will has a severe case of hay fever and asthma.

The weather has been very mild all during November. It is raining a little tonight. We were planning on going to Millers tomorrow for Thanksgiving. We had hoped to make ice cream but can't get the ice on account of the weather. I have been sick all day. My stomach has been off for two or three weeks. Will is busy on the books for the farm and the town. We will stay home for our Thanksgiving. Soon we will be preparing for Christmas.

Will and I lived in the house in Millard for the rest of our lives. For fifty-six years Will held the elected position of clerk of Sugar Creek Township. Every afternoon, for decades, Will walked to the corner store to get the evening newspaper. On a February afternoon in 1959, as he walked home at dusk, he was struck by a car and killed in front of our house. He was eighty-six.

I lived alone in the house for another year. I spent my final days and months at the Homestead Convalescent Hospital in Delavan. Our house in Millard, our well-lived-in house, stands in disrepair with the appearance of abandonment. You can remember us, Will and me, living day and night those many years together.

Seventeen
Nothing Is Lost

We wake up in the morning after a night of dreaming. An adjustment quickly follows bringing us into the waking state that we know as ourselves. Each morning is a new creation of our being, of who we think we are in mind and body, and name. You could not entertain your scattered state for more than a few seconds without vertigo and disturbing confusion. You put the pieces together for another day. And you wonder if you still are the person you were before the night began.

King Richard II experiences the annihilation of the self at the end of Shakespeare's play. "When time is broke and no proportion kept!" Time has laid waste to his known existence. How many times, how often, do we have to put ourselves together to maintain proportion, to go on with our lives? What would it be for us to entertain brief moments of the true state of our nature? With words addressed to the Buddha, Thich Nhat Hanh writes, "I shall listen to your advice and look deeply into impermanence, interdependence, emptiness, and interbeing in order to arrive at the deep realization that all that exists has the nature of no birth and no death, no coming and no going, no being and no nonbeing, no permanence and no annihilation." Nothing that exists has a separate reality. Everything is interdependent and a part of everything else. At some absolute level, beyond our human calculations, nothing is lost. This is how we can think of all things, flashing across the dreams of our existence.

All things, including us, are made of other things. Nothing has a separate existence, a separate self. We are, still and always, made of our parents and grandparents and all the ancestors before. We have all descended from the first humans that appeared in Africa and moved in subsequent generations to other continents. And before these people, we humans had evolved from primates, and the primates had evolved from early mammals. Our origins, human and otherwise, go back billions of years to the single cell organisms growing in moist places. And before all this, we came from the matter — never to be lost — of the universe. We have been here from the beginning.

In a comprehensive family genealogy, we all are related to each other. We are related not only to the relatives of the familial categories but also to all beings before us, and to those who will exist after our time. We are more than our family tree, related to everyone, on the tree and off. And ultimately we are connected to, we are, the matter of the cosmos. We are not alone; we are everywhere, then and now and always. Let us entertain the sweet music of the universe. Nothing is lost.

Eighteen
I Shot an Arrow into the Air

LET THE DAY BEGIN with a valentine heart. A heart that is pierced by cupid's arrow, an arrow of love heightened with passion. This image is of classical proportions, of the gods and goddesses of ancient times. And in early Christian time, the priest Saint Valentine would die in prison with a note to the guard's daughter, signed, "Love from your Valentine."

For a long time we have sought the words and symbols to express this longing of the heart. This deep longing to be connected to others, to know the connection in our daily lives. Much depends on the heart, this vital organ of body and soul. The heart that is true, never false. With Shakespeare's first line of the sonnet: "O never say that I was false of heart."

From down at the old place, a valentine card came to me the first year of my life. Great-Aunt Kate sent cupid to pierce my heart with the arrow of love. An entry that lasted, never to heal, a love that would overcome any death. The bow was drawn and love was delivered certainly forever.

Attend this day carefully to the practice of love. The love and compassion for others and for oneself. Help others to transform their suffering, where there is suffering, into a love that recognizes our interdependence, the essence of our being. The heart pierced by love. Thus have I heard and thus have I seen. As real a dream as ever I will know.

In the field, from planting time to harvest, you could hear my father reciting the lines from Henry Wadsworth Longfellow's poem:

> I shot an arrow into the air,
> It fell to earth I knew not where.
> For, so swiftly it flew, the sight
> Could not follow it in its flight.

You will find the poem printed in most country schoolbooks as the nineteenth century passed into the twentieth. The remaining stanzas:

> I breathed a song into the air,
> It fell to earth, I knew not where;
> For who has sight so keen and strong,
> That it can follow the flight of song?

> Long, long afterward, in an oak
> I found the arrow, still unbroke;
> And the song, from beginning to end,
> I found again in the heart of a friend.

My father, as with the poet, is telling all who will hear that those things of long ago still exist even when they are out of our sight. That which once was still is.

Such is the search for love as cupid's arrow speeds through air and time. With heart in song, the arrow goes to uncertain destination. But the arrow in flight may be enough when one is young. Only after many years does the poet, and the one who recites the poem, know that the arrow of love sent in song, a song still heard, is unbroken and has landed. A life, in the field with the oak still standing, has found its perfect mark. What is sown in the springtime will reach harvest.

They shared a song, my mother and father, many songs. You will see, years later, the albums they created out of love for this family. There is no dividing line between living and dreaming. What you love and sing about and dream about are one and the same. There is no life without the dreaming. Life is the manifestation of dreams.

On the cover of the black scrapbook is a picture of a Scotsman standing on a rock and blowing a horn with his hound at this side. Inside on the first page is the clipping from the newspaper: "A son, Earl Richard, was born Wednesday, May 16, to Mr. and Mrs. Floyd Quinney at Walworth County Hospital." The year is 1934, and a card announces my arrival — "Hello Everybody!" Another card, from neighboring cousins, notes that the baby will "make home a little heaven on earth." Pages follow filled with cards from far and near of love and best wishes to the child born to this family.

The design and artwork found on the pages of the scrapbook express the aesthetics of the time.

Cousin Vera in Canada sends the first Easter card to the baby. The first birthday is observed with many cards from relatives, friends, and neighbors. "Happy Birthday to a Little Man," says the card from neighbor Bernice:

Here's a Birthday wish
For a little lad
For the happiest day
He has ever had

And another year comes with greetings for another birthday and the holidays. More valentine cards, one of a boy playing an accordion that pops out of the card. The message on the card is of the power of song: *The Same Old Tune Keeps Coming Out: The Words Are "I Love You."*

The things we place into the world live on long after we lose sight of them. Appearing again as artifacts found in attics and basements of old houses or, perhaps, preserved in the historical archives. These are the shards from the past. Watching yet another performance of Hamlet, we are reminded that there may be life beyond a void of the great unknown. Hamlet, at the death scene, tells Horatio, "The rest is silence," a silence for Hamlet. He has told Horatio to tell the story:

If thou didst ever hold me in thy heart
Absent thee from felicity awhile,
And in this harsh world draw thy breath in pain,
To tell my story.

Someday the tale of the sweet prince will be told. "Horatio, I am dead; thou livest. Report me and my cause aright to the unsatisfied." Shakespeare's play will be read and performed for centuries hence. Not a void of nothingness when the tales are told another time. We are here, the living, bearing witness to the silenced lives. We are left to play the music and sing the songs.

Nineteen
The Teller of Tales

"Meanwhile, I scribble on." So wrote Arthur Crew Inman in his diary, a diary that began in 1919 and continued into 1963. The handwritten diary, consisting of 155 handwritten volumes, is one of the longest and most remarkable diaries ever written. The original volumes were taken from the vault of a Boston bank and edited by Daniel Aaron and published in two volumes by Harvard University in 1985.

In his darkened Boston apartment, Inman wrote an estimated seventeen million words that chronicle his life, the life of his wife, Evelyn, and the stories from the lives of at least a thousand people he knew and interviewed, as well as daily reflections — however biased — on national politics, wars and revolutions, and the social changes of the times. Inman wrote forthrightly about his fears, compulsions, fantasies, and nightmares. He rented the apartments above and below his own in Garrison Hall to shield himself from the outside noises.

The diary contains endless worries about the writer's health. According to some speculation, Inman suffered from temporal lobe epilepsy and may have had the condition known as hypergraphia. Anyone who has a great need to read and write daily might wonder if he or she is on the borderline of such a condition. The reading and writing daily without end, recording the dreams, giving a narrative to the dreams that dance day and night in our heads. Inman died in 1963 by a suicide that would silence the unbearable noise from the nearby construction of the Prudential Tower. It was a noise that could not be filtered out by his brain or by writing another entry in his diary.

How to start your day writing? First, there must be the need; otherwise you can be doing something else, living another way. I often think of Ernest Hemingway, of nearly a century ago, squeezing the peel of little oranges into the edge of the flame, waiting for the words to come. He walks to the window, looks over the roofs of Paris, and thinks to himself: "All you have to do is write one true sentence. Write the truest sentence that you know." Late in life, in his memoir, *A Moveable Feast,* he would tell us that writing stories when he was young in Paris was good and severe discipline. Writing is a way to understand your being in the world, to learn from it, and a way to go on.

In the middle of the seventeenth century, Matsuo Bashō, haiku poet of Japan, took to the open road in the spirit of Buddhist philosophy. He recorded his travels, sometimes published and titled as *Narrow Road to a Far Province.* Bashō reminds us that life itself is a journey: "Those who steer a boat across the sea, or drive a horse over the earth till they succumb to the weight of years, spend every minute of their lives traveling." This guiding idea is found throughout the Western canon, as well, in such classical works as *The Odyssey, The Pilgrim's Progress,* and *The Canterbury Tales.*

For me, in various travels and writings, photographs would be my poems. And I would be the teller of tales. Sometimes, still, I wake up in the morning from dreaming that I am young and ready to begin a great adventure. One of my earliest inspirations came from reading the autobiography of the explorer and paleontologist Roy Chapman Andrews, *Under a Lucky Star*. I was a freshman in high school in Delavan, in 1948, and I had been browsing in Abrams Public Library in town, before driving home for evening chores. I took from the shelf the book with the brown and yellow jacket that pictured a camel caravan crossing the Gobi Desert. I learned immediately that the author was born and grew up just a few miles away, in Beloit. If a boy from Wisconsin, from my part of Wisconsin, could become an explorer and discoverer of dinosaur eggs in Mongolia, what might be possible for me? The autobiography is regarded as one of the best science books ever written. "From the time that I can remember anything I always intended to be an explorer," Chapman wrote. He has been an inspiration to me throughout my life, and continues to be a source for the adventures of everyday life. This life of the explorer, and teller of tales, has been an inspiration for a life of writing.

Twenty
When We Were Cowboys

THE REVERIES, mine being those of a cowboy, dispel any doubt that we live in a dream world. Cows grazing in the pasture on summer days; milking the cows in the barn early mornings in the winter; on my horse rounding up the cattle at the end of the field. Throughout the summer, after chores and supper, my brother and I would listen to the latest episode of *The Lone Ranger.* We would ride our bicycles on the dusty road imagining ourselves on the range pursuing outlaws and rescuing maidens. All summer I would feed and groom a Jersey or Holstein heifer to be shown at the county fair at the end of summer. A box of prize ribbons is stored someplace among the treasures.

This day I have spent listening to cowboy songs. It all began early in the morning when I heard on the radio a recording of the traditional cowboy song "The Old Chisholm Trail." The song was being sung by Tex Ritter:

> Come along boys and listen to my tale
> I'll tell you of my troubles on the old Chisholm Trial
> Come a ti yi yippy, come a tee yi yay
> Ti yi yippy yi yay

Come all you cow punchers, come along with me on the old Chisholm Trail.

An early recorded version of the song was by Huddie Ledbetter (Lead Belly) and was titled "When I Was a Cowboy." Cowboys of various origins working on ranches in the Southwest created the tradition of cowboy songs. The cowboy songs "Home on the Range" and "Get Along Little Dogies" were collected by Alan Lomax from a retired black trail cook in 1908. Many of the cowboy songs were a reworking of older folk ballads that came from England, Ireland, and Scotland. Songs soothed the cattle and kept the cowboys awake and alert through the long night.

The historical cowboy lasted only until the 1890s. But the romantic myth of the cowboy would never go away. The ballads of cowboy life — ranging from the brooding songs about death, songs of herding cattle and nights around the campfire, humorous songs and tales of chases and gunfights — added to the poetry and music of American culture. The cowboy myth spread around the world. Buffalo Bill Cody toured Europe with his Wild West Show, reenacting the winning of the West and portraying the conquest of Native Americans.

The herds of longhorn cattle had doubled in size during the Civil War and were roaming the ranges of the Southwest. Though of little value in Texas, cattle were in demand as beef in the cities of the North. This was the golden era of rounding up, herding, and

driving cattle to the stockyards in Abilene, Cheyenne, and Kansas City. New railroad lines carried the cattle to Omaha and Chicago and to the cities of the East.

The first trail used for cattle drives, sometimes following the earlier Indian trails, was the Chisholm Trail. Hundreds of cowboys drove several million head of cattle over the trail. And countless versions of "The Old Chisholm Trail" were sung — in the saddle, around the campfire, and in the saloons along the way. You can still hear recordings of it by popular singers Gene Autry, Woody Guthrie, Roy Rogers, and Michael Martin Murphey. Classic western movies like *The Texans* and *Red River* portrayed the cattle drives over the Chisholm Trail.

Many were the tales and laments of cowboys driving cattle in all kinds of weather, across rivers and streams, into canyons and over mountains and through badlands, and fighting off rustlers and Indians. "Feet in the stirrups and seat in the saddle, I hung and rattled with them longhorn cattle." The cowboy hopes someday to quit herding cattle.

There is always a horse with a cowboy. Riding bareback on "Sparkplug," I rode into the sunset before bedtime imagining that I was a cowboy. Grandfather Quinney made part of his living "breaking" mustangs from Wyoming into plow horses in Wisconsin. Horses were in the blood of the Irish fleeing the famine. Far from the Wild West, we rode and worked with horses and imagined that we were cowboys. Harnesses, horse collars, bridles, and ropes hung in the barn ready for work the next morning. A bridle hangs, still, in the doorway as I pass to the garage of my house in town.

There was a horse — a racehorse — that was made famous in the ballad "Stewball" (sometimes called "Skewball"). The ballad dates back to the eighteenth century in Ireland and England. The horse, in the race of two, triumphed by either the stumbling of the gray mare or being the faster horse in the race. Coming to America in the nineteenth century, the song was sung by slaves and became widely known as a chain-gang song. Lead Belly, Woody Guthrie, Pete Seeger, and Peter, Paul, and Mary have sung versions of it. I listen closely today to Joan Baez's haunting rendition from the sixties. "Stewball was a good horse. He wore his head high."

The other song that will fill the day is "Ballad of the Absent Mare" by Leonard Cohen. Beginning the song, Cohen sings, "Say a prayer for the cowboy, his mare's run away." To my surprise, I have just learned that the ballad is based on the twelfth-century allegory of oxherding, the Zen instruction for enlightenment. Classically, the boy — the herder of the ox — searches for the ox only to discover that the ox was never missing. The ox is within the herder, the Buddha nature being in all of us. In Cohen's ballad, the mare is found, tamed, and the rider no longer needs the rein. Finally, a return to the source, equanimity, enlightenment: "And they're gone like the smoke and they're gone like this song."

Twenty-One
I Thought about You

THINKING ABOUT THE FUTURE and the past takes place in the present. The only real time is the present moment; all else is a construct of what might be in the future or what is imagined as having been in the past. Being mindful in the present is being attentive and alive to the moment. Mindfulness gives birth to understanding, compassion, and love. With mindfulness, we are capable of enjoying all the wonders of life.

In my solitude, these days of the week when I am home alone, much of my present time is of things in the past, of people and relations, especially of family. The past is created anew in the process of writing. I am in time present as I write about things of the past.

Thinking freely in solitude moves the writer to unforeseen, unanticipated realms. Thinking in solitude is more than talk internalized, and more than the spoken word. Thinking takes place before speaking, before the shaping of thought into the verbal symbols that we know as the words of speech. A tape recording of the thoughts in your head would be quite different from a recording of your spoken words. Much is lost in talking, in speaking outside the solitude of thinking.

And yet, to be certain, these thoughts are not separate from the thoughts of others. Just as we are not separate selves, not separated from others, our thoughts are a part of all thoughts that are going on at the moment. We humans are of a collective consciousness and, likely, of the consciousness of other species, and of inanimate objects as well. There is the interpenetration of everything in the world. There is no separate existence — even (and especially) in our solitude. In solitude, we experience the oneness of all. Our connection to everything that exists, has ever existed, and that will exist in the future is mindfully understood in our moments of solitude. Then we know that we are not alone. It is then that I think about you.

What would a time of solitude be like if you did not know that it can and will end? Solveig returns from work at the end of each day. Each day I know that my solitude will be rounded with the pleasure of its ending. I spend much of my time alone, at this time in my life, but seldom am I lonely. Circumstances, beyond imagination, could change this. Blessed I am for this present time.

Without plan, spontaneously, the dial is turned and the day begins with a lyric about taking these chains from this heart and setting it free. This while I wait for the call from my brother that the electroconversion of his heart has been safely completed. After the call from the hospital last night that cardiopulmonary resuscitation had been administered when his heart had nearly failed.
 And I wait for my own appointment with a cardiologist today to learn the results of the CT scan determining if the aneurism on my aorta has expanded or remained the same since last year

this time. So much depends upon the heart, life itself. Listen to your heart and you know intimately your connection to every heart that beats this moment. As the heart beats, you know that you are not alone.

The light in the late afternoon sky signals the coming of spring. Among the ancients, the arrival of the vernal equinox indicated that a new year was about to begin. Nature would obey as flowers and grasses emerged from the ground and birds began to sing. Here, this morning, little more than a week before the equinox, snow falls gently, cardinals and sparrows come to the feeder, and a squirrel gathers a few kernels from the deck. My brother and I, in towns apart, thank an ancient god for life here on earth.

You try to absorb the deeper view of what life is. Beginning with the insight that all life is impermanent, and that impermanence is a positive fact that can be understood positively. Impermanence gives life its value and promotes our compassion for one another. Thich Nhat Hanh writes: "When we accept that all things are impermanent, we will not be incapacitated by suffering when things decay and die. We can remain peaceful and content in the face of continuity and change, prosperity and decline, success and failure."

The deeper view of life goes in and out of focus regularly as I live thankfully each day. Being human, we dream that we might escape the fate — the promise — of impermanence and death. Everlasting life will depend on another dream.

The Diamond Sutra ends with the observation that all composed things are like a dream. Throughout the sutra, the discourse between Subhuti and the Buddha is on being a compassionate person whose intention is to relieve our own suffering and the suffering of our fellow beings. The person on the way to enlightenment, helping others, is called a *bodhisattva*. The bodhisattva does not have a separate identity: "Bodhisattvas will have no perception of an egoistic self, neither of a separate entity nor of a soul, no perception of a personality. Nor will they even have a perception of dharma or non-dharma, for in them there will be neither perception nor non-perception." In the heart of the bodhisattva there exists great energy called *bodhicitta*. Many people can be helped — with suffering relieved — by those who aspire to the life of the bodhisattva. All beings, we are told in the sutra, have the potential to be on the path of enlightenment and compassion. The vow is to relieve the suffering of all living beings, where peace may be realized.

Thus you have heard that all things of the mind are to be regarded as fleeting images. If you look deeply into things you will be able to be free of illusion. We live our ordinary lives knowing that all composed things are like a dream, that with compassion we can be of help to others, and that the absolute realm is one of selflessness and impermanence. Share these fruits with all beings.

Twenty-Two
The Leisure of an Elderly Present

THE SANSKRIT WORD *sunyata* is often translated into English as "emptiness." It could also be translated as "everything." Either way, the reference is to dependent origination of all phenomena. The mind creates a world of apparent separation and independence. The absolute reality is sunyata.

In the book and commentary on the Diamond Sutra from the Pythagorean Sangha, edited by Raghavan Iyer, we read the eighteenth-century verse from the Seventh Dalai Lama. On being mindful of sunyata:

> All through the circle of apparent and transitory objects
> Spreads the space of the clear light of the real, the ultimate.
> In which all things have a transcendental being.
> Forsaking all mental inventions.
> Dwell in the pure state of sunyata.
> Draw in your mind, centering it in the real.
> Guide your attention with mindfulness.
> Holding it within the real.

Sometimes, with great care, we may dwell in the pure state of sunyata.

As we age, we may release ourselves from the pursuit of being immersed in the daily events of the world, locally and globally. We may come to think that it is not necessary to be up-to-date on everything that is happening in the world. That being informed and engaged is not necessarily a moral imperative at this time of life. I take heart this day from a decision made by the writer Doris Grumbach during her days of solitude: "I wanted to shield myself from as much of the terrible particulars of modern existence as possible to preserve my shrinking time for, well, let me say it, pompous as it sounds, contemplation of more important questions, of generalities based on a past I have stored away for review in the leisure of an elderly present." Many of the horrifying details of the present were held at arm's length as the wonders of solitude were being explored. And for a while, the writer notes, "without the constant presence of violence in my consciousness I knew who I was."

It is reported that when a monk asked the Buddha what is meant by the world being empty, he replied, "Insofar as it is empty of a self or anything pertaining to a self." Nothing has a separate existence, an identity of its own. Although we perceive of a world of concrete and discrete things, these things are empty of a substance and identity of their own. Beyond the conditioned mind, in the realm of the absolute, everything is part of everything else. How could we be alone when we too are everything?

Twenty-Three
The Way of Everyday Life

THE SNOW MELTS DAILY and green shoots of grass are appearing with the warming sun. Beyond the vernal equinox, days are longer than the nights. Late in the afternoon, the turkey vultures soar and circle before roosting for the night. As nature's harvesters, the vultures clean the earth of the spoils of winter. Behold, a new season is upon us.

Each spring I read again Sterling North's book of springtime vignettes, *Hurry, Spring!* Written late in his life, the book is filled with remembrances of spring when he was growing up in Wisconsin. The migratory return of birds, the awakening of mammals, the flowing of rivers, the granting of one more spring. North reminds us that spring on this continent comes northward at about fifteen miles a day, starting in southern Florida in February and reaching us here in the Middle West this time of year. You could follow spring, as once did naturalist Edward Way Teale, mile by mile, day by day.

A great gray owl, the largest of owls, has flown out of its far northern range and sits on a branch of a tall spruce tree at the western edge of town. Watchers of birds gather daily with binoculars and cameras to record this unusual sighting. Likely this is a juvenile of its species, not yet attached to a mate, in search of food in short supply this spring in Canada. Eyes beam from the large gray facial disc, an imposing presence as we watch from the street. I will keep watch daily until this great gray owl takes flight in pursuit of its own destiny.

In the meantime, I will continue my reading of the Zen writings of Dōgen, the Japanese Buddhist teacher of the thirteenth century. My own pursuit — a flight often taken — of a better understanding and personal integration of dependent origination: Everything is interconnected; everything affects everything else; nothing exists independently of other beings and phenomena. All things and all beings are the way they are because they are connected to all other things and beings. I am dependent on the great gray owl as it is dependent on me. Our flights and our returns are of the same Dharma.

I study and practice Zen because enlightenment is nothing other than the study and practice of Zen. This Dōgen taught in the compiled writings we know as *Shōbōgenzō:* Practice and enlightenment are one and the same. We — among all things and all beings — are endowed with Dharma, with the absolute reality that transcends our conditioned existence. Spiritual practice itself is enlightenment, the realization of Dharma — absolute reality.

Absolute reality, in hermeneutical study, is sometimes the alternative concept for God or the Divine. Without anthropomorphic presumption, absolute reality is the source through which all things and beings emanate. This reality is in contrast to the relative reality of a finite, humanly constructed, reality. Absolute reality is the un-

conditional reality that transcends the conditioned mind. It is a return — in practice and enlightenment — to the source of all being. I will rest with the conclusion that absolute reality is already present and, being so, is not to be sought elsewhere in places other than daily life. Living daily is my practice and my enlightenment.

In his commentary on Dōgen, Francis H. Cook in his book *Sounds of Valley Streams* notes that one finishes reading *Shōbōgenzō* with the feeling that something of great richness, depth, and scope has been completed. He compares Dōgen's teaching and writing with the Greek tragedies, Walt Whitman's *Leaves of Grass*, Herman Melville's *Moby Dick,* and Henry David Thoreau's *Walden.* Something very important has been conveyed, and the reader is left with a lingering sense of completion and inevitability.

Dōgen's answer to the question of what happens after we die is grounded on impermanence and the absence of a substantial self. There is no self to survive death; what happens with death is an entirely different state, not a different state of the same thing. Impermanence is not a matter of things changing, as one getting older, for instance. Cook writes: "True impermanence is grasped when we perceive that anything, material or psychic, is what it is for a brief moment, ceases to be, and is replaced by a novel state." This is the emptiness of things — the Dharma, the way things are. One's present state of being is followed by a different state. Each of us is a perfect expression of absolute reality.

Dōgen taught that fish swim in the water and birds fly in the sky. We all have our place and path in absolute reality. Our place and path must be our own ordinary life. Cook thus writes, "The way of practice and the door to truth consequently lie beneath our feet." This ordinary life, otherwise seen as mundane and ordinary, is sacred and holy. Absolute reality is in the actual living of each day. Before this day ends, I will go to the tall spruce at the edge of town and watch the great gray owl as it watches me.

Twenty-Four
Field Notes

THE WORDS OF THE POET came again as I woke up in the morning: "Some day you will be one of those who lived long ago." At bedtime I had noted carefully the need to meditate on the absolute reality of emptiness. On staying in touch with life as it truly is, on realizing the interdependence of all things. This is the practice that is necessary in times of suffering and in the passing of all cherished things and beings. That peace may be as unending as land and sea.

Sterling North suffered a series of strokes late in life, yet he continued correspondence and completed his book on the coming of spring. Amazingly, we are told, he tapped out on the typewriter with a single finger his final book, *The Wolfling: A Documentary Novel of the Eighteen-Seventies.*

North was born in 1906 on a farm on the western edge of Lake Koshkonong. I pass this widening of the Rock River as I drive to my family farm in Walworth County. His grandparents had settled North's farm in the 1840s. *The Wolfling* is based on the boyhood experiences of North's father.

Next to the North farm was the eighty acres of the Thure Kumlien family. Thure Kumlien (1819–1888) had emigrated from Sweden after being taught by the successor to Linnaeus and graduating from Uppsala University with honors. He married the woman that he had met at the university shortly after they arrived in Wisconsin. They lived in a log cabin they built on the newly purchased eighty acres of woods and wetlands. Kumlien would become a noted naturalist, teaching at nearby Albion Academy and identifying and collecting the animal and plant species of the region.

In *The Wolfling*, Sterling North's father, identified as the boy Robbie Trent, roams the woodlands and the marshes with Kumlien, and learns the love of nature from him. With beautiful narration, North portrays what the boy learned from the naturalist. The coming of spring, for example:

> The boy knew from what he had been told by Professor Kumlien that the miracle of spring was due to the tilt of the earth, and the greater abundance of sunlight now lavished upon the Northern Hemisphere. This light and warmth first melted the snows of winter. It sent a stir of life into the seeds and roots of grass and flowers, pulled the sweet sap of the sugar maples to the very tips of the budding branches. It stimulated the water birds and songsters into their seasonal migration northward, and told the wolves and many other animals that it was time to mate and to bring forth their young.

The boy labored for his father on the farm, and received an education in nature from his neighbor Kumlien.

At the farm, when I was growing up, we listened in April for the first calls of the frogs in the pond down at the old place where my ancestors made their home after emigrating from Ireland.

The peeping and the croaking sounds came to us loud and clear as the days grew warmer. The red-winged blackbirds returned to the pond and perched on cattails as mating territories were established. Mallards returned for nesting along the edge of the pond. Tadpoles began to swim in the shallow water, and the grasses shot up all around the pond. The red buds of the silver maples appeared early and eventually the leaves emerged. With scant time to linger and observe, spring was bringing the days that meant the beginning of work in the fields. The tilling, the planting, and the cultivating would follow as the summer progressed. The season of harvest would complete the cycle for another year.

In the world of nature at the farm, I gained much of my education, spiritual sustenance, and hope. The realization that life was becoming complex and mysterious was a gift given to me by our neighbor Burton Hanson. Sometime midway in the 1940s, Burton and his wife, Gladys, rented the house on what we called the Dutcher Place, the land and set of buildings that my father and mother had purchased a few years earlier. Next to my parents and relatives, Burton became the most important adult in my life. He was the person who brought me close to nature. Returning from one of his trips north, he brought me a section of a birch tree that had been chewed by a beaver. A treasure I still keep.

Burton took my brother and me fishing many evenings after a long day of work in the fields. Along Turtle Creek, we fished for bullheads and bluegills. Catching fish was incidental to walking along the banks of the creek and watching the evening come to

the marsh. "Man alive," Burton would exclaim whenever one of us caught a large fish, and when the setting sun lit up the evening sky.

Burton had skills that were in short supply as the 1940s gave way to the postwar years. He was what some called a "handyman" who could repair or build almost anything. Burton would tell me, "Anyone can make something, but a good carpenter is one who can repair his mistakes." One summer I worked with Burton, and together we built a handsome pig house on a farm several miles away.

The old farmhouse that Burton and Gladys lived in looked to the west over the woods at the edge of the marsh. Before the settlers moved into southern Wisconsin, the area had been home to Indian tribes. Arrowheads were found when my father plowed the field next to the marsh. There appeared to be burial mounds on the oak knoll. Burton would look longingly into the marsh and the woods from his house on the hill.

A few letters passed between us after I left the farm, but I eventually lost contact with Burton. I visited him once in the house he had moved to in a western suburb of Chicago after Gladys died and he had remarried. The last time I saw him was on the day of my father's funeral. Burton stood with the others for the brief time at the graveside with tears in his eyes. Afterward, in the falling snow, we both retreated to parked cars over the hill. We had not tried to speak to each other. We were now beyond the solace of words.

Twenty-Five
Narrow Road to the Interior

Bashō, the pilgrim-poet of the seventeenth century, set out walking on a journey to the remote province of Japan's main island. On the five-month journey, he kept a record of his travel. His diary, variously translated and titled *Narrow Road to the Interior,* has become a classic of Japanese literature. I have lived a good portion of my life as a pilgrim inspired by Bashō's journey to the far province.

It is the middle of April. The spring season is making unsteady entrance. The weekly weather forecast has been of rain and snow and sleet. Yet, the sun shines through the clouds almost daily. Fog lifts in the morning and a new day, different from the one before, unfolds uncertainly. So much the better for exploring the uncharted terrain. I fill my fountain pen, wipe ink from fingers, and write a few words across the page. A journey on paper as if walking over wooded hills and through boggy marshes.

My mother died fourteen years ago today. On a Thursday morning, much like this morning, Solveig and I drove north across the Illinois-Wisconsin border with plans to take my mother to see her doctor. We arrived at the farm finding that she had spent the night in the living room chair unable to reach the bedroom. She had waited the night for our help, and passed away shortly after we arrived. I held her hand in the last moments, still hoping that we would be able to go to the emergency room at the hospital in time to save her life.

You are told that you will grieve, and that in time the grieving will go away. For me, and I know for my brother as well, the grieving will never end. Grieving is remembering deeply, and recognizing that our mother is still with us as we live our daily lives. You may find some solace in the practice of impermanence and the absolute reality of selflessness, a practice that assures us that we all remain together.

Even leaving our friends for a while makes for a heavy heart. Bashō, knowing that this ephemeral world is an illusion, wept as he departed on his journey to the far province. He wrote a poetic line in his diary: "Eyes are wet with tears." Adding that he might as well be going to the ends of the earth.

Last night we watched in the concert hall as Willie Nelson and his band played and sang the songs that have spanned decades. Periods of my life have followed the lyrics of one song or another. Near the end of the evening, he sang "Funny How Time Slips Away."

> Well, it's been so long now
> But it seems now, that it was only yesterday
> Gee, ain't it funny how time just slips away?

We walked to the parking lot to retrieve the car for the return home. Encouraged by Willie Nelson's night of music, one song quickly following another, delivered powerfully this eightieth year of the singer's life.

The delicate and curious chipping sparrow is tapping at the window. Either for my attention or in recognition of itself in reflection. This sparrow with rufous crown will be my friend all spring and summer long. If the spiritual is being in touch with everything around and beyond us, my days with chipping sparrow will be spiritual days. In touch with one thing is to be in touch with everything. The ground of my being is known in the sight and sound of little chipping sparrow.

We watched the red fox cross the length of the yard. With spritely gait, the red fox is regarded as one of the most beautiful, yet peculiar animals walking the Earth. This fox among us has captured our imaginations and must be a resident making a home in a den in the ravine at the end of the street. He ventures through properties in search of food for mate and pups. Nocturnal by reputation, this fox is comfortable in the broad daylight of morning and afternoon. A neighbor recently saw the fox stretched out on the lawn basking in the sunshine. Our consciousness has increased with the presence of the red fox in our midst. I have placed three chicken eggs beneath the maple as invitation and sustenance for the passing fox.

Each graceful step of the fox brings me to the awareness of the sacredness of each present moment. There is peace and happiness and well-being as I give attention to the here and now. I see myself in connection to generations—ancestors and those to come—and to everything on Earth. My home territory, with red fox, is in every breath and step. With mindful watching, we recognize our true home.

The good news has come today of the birth of my first granddaughter. She will be named Aurelia. Names already in the families of Anne and Bryan will be middle names. The ancient name, Aurelia, from Roman times, will mark the lifetime of one so little now. "Golden" is the meaning of the name. She joins — she continues — the generations that make our human chain on this planet. We of the generations are intimately connected — of the same substance and life force. May we live carefully, mindfully, helping future generations realize enlightenment, love, and peace.

Today's newspaper carries the obituary for George Jones, proclaiming in the front-page headline, "His Life Was a Country Song." It has been nearly twelve years since the magical evening that we watched and listened to George Jones on stage at the Walworth County Fair. A full moon rose above the racetrack and climbed the far end of the grandstand as night fell and the show began. George Jones, with a fanfare from the Jones Boys, walked onto the stage to the enthusiastic applause and cheers of the crowd. We had secured our seats early, and had waited as the grandstand filled and the time neared for the appearance of the country star. With our friends Don and Sally we were about to see and hear the music of the great country musician.

All the years of writing songs, of performing, and of living a life were before us as the lights above the stage flashed from one color to another, ending in blue for the start of another slow number. The aging singer gracefully, and humorously, acknowledged his advancing years, working his life into the long list of songs for which he is known. The lyrical phrases of songs with just the right melodies, sung in a resonant voice that effortlessly moved from high notes to low, came one after another: *come take my hand — who's going to fill your shoes — sweet as strawberry wine — walk through this world with me — living and dying with the choices I've made — he stopped loving her today.*

When the singing was over, we slowly walked down the steps of the grandstand and left the fairgrounds, made our way to the center of town where we had parked our cars, and parted for home. I remember telling Don that we invest our heroes with qualities that we could not have in ourselves.

This morning I am dancing with the daffodils. Springing from the nooks and crannies of the yard are the golden heads truly marking the season. From my window above the yard, I am in reverie with William Wordsworth.

> For oft, when on my couch I lie
> In vacant or in pensive mood,
> They flash upon the inward eye
> Which is the bliss of solitude,
> And then my heart with pleasure fills,
> And dances with the daffodils.

The daffodils dance as I return to the making of a few words to the day.

Little Fyntan, two-year-old brother of baby Aurelia, has been given a doll and offered a gift from his new sister. The hospital staff provided these tokens of bonding as the family returned to their home in Memphis. Photographs have come to us daily on the computer screen.
  The stereo brings the haunting voice of George Jones.

> If you've ever looked up at a sky with no blue
> Then you've seen a picture of me without you

Another country song of lament that gives the heart the depth of life.

The day begins with a yodel. Patsy Montana is singing the song that we heard so often on the radio on a Saturday night from the WLS *National Barn Dance*. These many days and years later, I still want "to learn to rope and to ride." And, with the cowgirl singer, I want to ride over the plains and the desert, with wind in my face, hearing the sound of coyotes howling. Most of all, I still want to strum a guitar, and play and sing a country song. If you would ask me today what I think I am doing as I write these few words, I would tell you that I'm writing a country song.

In the evening, I am reading slowly, once again, the eloquent writing of novelist James Salter. His new novel, written late in life, has an epigraph of Salter's own making:

> There comes a time when you
> realize that everything is a dream,
> and only those things preserved in writing
> have any possibility of being real.

The protagonist of the novel is giving close attention to the course of his life, and to the memories of that life that remain in the telling.

This ordinary and everyday life that we remember is also the construction of a new dream. It is the memory — the composing of a memory — that is the new reality. With the Diamond Sutra before me daily, I know that memory — the writing of the memory — is also a dream. The work of the mind in reverie and reflection is no less compelling for being a dream. The dream is now the reality, as relative as that reality may be.

The temperature is nearing eighty degrees. Lunchtime and I am sitting at the table on the balcony. The eggs that I placed at the bottom of the yard are missing, taken by Mr. Fox we might assume. A robin swoops low over the garden. Migrating white-throated sparrows are feeding in the newly grown grass below. A large blue jay dashes among the branches of the locust tree. No doubts now about the certain arrival of spring with noontimes warmed by the sun.

A local brewery has brought a new brew to the shelves. An attractive and comical label graces the bottle, pirates raising a glass aboard a makeshift boat on a nearby lake. The text on the label invites us to the brew called "Scurvy."

> The pirates of Rock Lake. No cannon to thunder. Nothing to plunder. And the menacing schooners of yore have now been replaced by party barges. What's a modern-day pirate to do? Thankfully, skinny dipping has replaced walking the plank and there's still plenty of booty to be had.

An India pale ale brewed with orange peel and emitting citrus aroma. Oh a fine day it is.

Searching the Internet on my computer, I find more information about my aunt Marjorie, my father's sister that I never met. In the census for 1930, she is living in the household of a family in Evanston, Illinois. Her relation to the head of the house, William Williams, is listed as that of "Servant." She would have been thirty-five then.

The great experiment known as Prohibition ended in 1931. That year Marjorie became part owner of a business, purchasing with a friend the Shingle Inn located on Highway 14 a few miles south of Delavan. They ran the tavern, which had been a bootlegging operation during Prohibition, until Marjorie died unexpectedly in 1935 of a ruptured appendix. In probate court, bank funds amounted to $581.06, plus $35 in cash and a 1930 Ford coupe. Other material items of value consisted of liquor, tobacco and cigarettes, candy and nuts, glassware, two tables and six chairs, a radio, cash register, and a cabin with three beds.

Before the brief time of being part owner of the Shingle Inn, Marjorie had worked as a maid in houses around Delavan Lake, and for a while as a maid in the Wisconsin School for the Deaf in town. While other women of her age taught in country schools and married farmers, Marjorie took another direction. She has been, for me all my life, a woman of mystery and inspiration. In a photograph from her album, Marjorie stands at the old place, dressed in fine clothes, and looks toward the farm in the distance. For many years I have kept a framed portrait of Marjorie on my desk.

By the looks of things, this will be a rain-filled day. Wet, and gray, and I am happy enough. In the background, Waylon Jennings is singing "My Heroes Have Always Been Cowboys." Sharon Vaughn wrote the lyrics during her Nashville days. Willie Nelson sings the song on the soundtrack of Robert Redford's film *The Electric Horseman.* Great resonance midway in the song this day: "Cowboys are special with their own brand of misery from being alone too long." This is neither a complaint nor a lament as a gentle rain keeps falling.

Tonight an excursion to the Office Depot store for a few writing supplies. Searching in the aisle for a three-ring binder, having outgrown the current one as this manuscript gets larger, I'm greeted by a tall man coming from the other direction. He stops me and begins a conversation on the advantages of the Twist-Erase mechanical pencil with the 0.9 lead. I tell him that this is the same pencil that I use, not for writing but for underlining and making marginal notes when I am reading a book, and for occasional notes. He asks me about my writing and, following me to the checkout counter, tells me about the book he is writing on beavers. The beaver nearly became extinct as it was trapped for the making of hats. He has been working on this project for many years, and purchased a box of 1500 sheets of printer paper, and convinced me to do the same. I'm sorry that we didn't exchange names.

Bashō, in his *Knapsack Notebook,* translated by Sam Hamill, expounds on the art of the travel journal. He tell us that it is easy to observe the mundane — overcast skies in the morning becoming sunny in the afternoon. He writes, "Nothing's worth noting that is not seen with fresh eyes." But even Bashō's random observations and experiences along the way — in a secluded house in the mountains or in a lonely inn — linger in the mind and heart of the reader. Our observations can touch and stir the heart and mind of the reader. Bashō observes this about his writing:

> I write in my notebook with the intention of stimulating good conversation, hoping that it will also be of use to some fellow traveler. But perhaps my notes are mere drunken chatter, the incoherent babbling of a dreamer. If so, read them as such.

With Bashō, we are in good company as we travel and make our notes about what we have seen and what we have thought.

Poet Lucien Stryk passed away earlier this year. He was a practitioner and noted translator of Zen poetry. He wrote the straightforward and direct poems of everyday life, focusing on simple and familiar details. Born in Poland in 1924, he soon moved to Chicago with his family. He studied at several universities, served in World War II, taught for years at Northern Illinois University, and was a poet all his life. I was fortunate to be a colleague of his and, in an adult course he taught, I was given kind and generous encouragement. In our town amid the cornfields, Lucien was the sage and poet.

Included in his book of new and collected poems, *And Still Birds Sing,* published in 1998, is a modern Japanese haiku poem (by Santoka) that was translated by Lucien — the haiku simple, elegant, mundane, and transcendental:

> To the end of time,
> journeying,
> cutting toe-nails.

Our human journey to the end of time; our personal journey in the course of a lifetime. Life truly is a journey as we attend daily to the requirements of body and soul. What more could there be?

The weather forecast on the radio as I woke up this morning: "We will have an awfully pleasant day in Wisconsin." Awfully pleasant now as Les Brown's band plays its version of Johnny Mercer's "Dream." I think of the lyrics as the band plays on:

> So dream when the day is through
> Dream and they might come true
> Things never are as bad as they seem
> So dream, dream, dream.

Dream when you're feeling blue, and dream when things are awfully pleasant too.

So much is invested in the possibility of dreams. We dream our lives into being. Our dreams become the realities of our lives.

Horse-drawn buggies were coming toward us as we neared the small town of Kingston. We must have met at least twenty on Sunday afternoon as we passed the well-kept farms of Amish families. Solveig and I had spent the day in Ripon visiting my brother and his family.

Calling my brother later, I was informed that the Amish do not have church buildings. Services are held at various households. A large white wagon carries chairs and pews from house to house. The wagon is parked at the front of the house for a week or more, and then pulled to the next house where services will be held during the week. Services last most of the day, led by local members, and there are programs for children and there is Bible study. Meals are prepared and served. Most of the church funds are to help members in times of need.

The day of travel passed as all things pass in this dream world of ours. At night, before turning off the bedside light, I read a meditation on impermanence prepared by Thich Nhat Hanh:

> Touching impermanence deeply, we touch the world beyond permanence and impermanence. We touch the ground of being, and see that what we have called "being" and "nonbeing" are just notions. Nothing is ever lost. Nothing is ever gained.

A day of being reminded that even the impermanence that we experience is an illusion. There is a reality beyond our notions of permanence and impermanence, an absolute reality where nothing is lost and nothing is gained.

I've received a package in the mail from my poet friend Mark Vinz containing his latest book of poems. When needing to read a poem about living in this midland that we share, I turn regularly to one of the poems in his book *Long Distance*. The poem "Directions" has a middle stanza on the sense of place in traveling.

My father couldn't understand the
trouble I had with directions. Every time
I'm lost I think of him, the country sense
I never had — the way he always knew
just where we were, the quickest routes,
the name of every crop in those mysterious
fields, and where to find the best cafés.

Mark and I each have an ever-expanding file of our correspondence over many years. Letters about our families, our travels, the weather, our writing, and of the inspiration and help we are giving each other. About ten years ago I traveled to his university in Minnesota to give a lecture on writing about and photographing the Midwest. With other writers from the English department, we spent an evening in a hotel bar and restaurant across the Red River in Fargo. We often remind each other of that evening, and last year in a letter I reminded Mark of the lyrics in Lyle Lovett's song "Farther Down the Line."

So let's have a hand for that young cowboy
And wish him better luck next time
And hope we see him up in Fargo
Or somewhere farther down the line

Mark wrote back right away letting me know that he recently had attended a magnificent concert by Lovett in a theater just down the line from Fargo.

Twenty-Six
When Words Come

A MID-MAY MORNING, as it is now, when Bashō begins his journey on the narrow road to the interior. The year, for Bashō, is 1689, three hundred and twenty-four years ago. With brush in hand, he writes these words in his journal: "A few old friends had gathered in the night and followed along far enough to see me off from the boat. Getting off at Senju, I felt three thousand miles rushing through my heart, the whole world only a dream. I saw it through farewell tears." He then composes the first haiku of the journey.

> Spring passes,
> and the birds cry out — tears
> in the eyes of fishes.

He begins his journey with the sorrow of departure. "Those who remain behind watch the shadow of a traveler's back disappear."

These words that we write across the page, where do they come from, and why? There is much speculation on the origin of the words that make a language for us. We could just as well add the idea that words fostered the evolution of our ability to walk upright. Much depends upon words, and on the placing of words in a sequence to form sentences. And with a few sentences, the writer constructs the unit we call a paragraph. Then paragraphs into chapters, and at some point, a completion that is a book or a journal between covers. Or a manuscript that is placed in a drawer or closet, perhaps to be forgotten forever.

What was important at the beginning was the need and desire to begin the writing of words. Writing words on a tablet, a wall, or on paper when speaking was not enough. Possibly the intent was to leave a message, a message that we were here. Words to signal that we, indeed, once existed.

And sometimes there might be a story to tell. A story that is as much myth as it is historical or current event. A story that tells us what it is to be human and living this life. The writing of a story is the composing of a dream.

A beautiful sight this morning, sunlight streaming across the table. My feast for the morning: fountain pens and pencils laid out, a bottle of blue ink, a stack of books, the three-ring notebook opened to a blank ruled page, scissors and glue stick, magnifying glass, and coffee in a nicely thrown and glazed pottery cup. No need to test blood pressure with nearby monitor.

The purple orchid is silhouetted in the window. Jay, cardinal, and the newly arrived catbird are perched on the feeder as squirrel jumps from tree to the balcony. Comforting thoughts of friends and family. My brother will return home from the hospital today. One song listened to this morning, "The Lark Ascending" by Ralph Vaughn Williams. *The New York Times* waits to be read sometime during the day. I've posted on the wall a quote by Emerson: "I cannot remember the books I've read any more than the meals I have eaten; even so, they have made me." Below, the garden has been prepared for planting. Nothing more needs to be written today.

The Dalai Lama is in town this week. There will be a public lecture — titled "In Praise of Dependent Origination" — for an audience of thousands, and sessions on consciousness and brain research at the university, and meditation with monks at the Deer Park Buddhist Center. A Tibetan prayer wheel filled with millions of mantras is being installed at the Center. Each rotation will provide personal purification and spread blessings to the world.

To live one's everyday life naturally and spontaneously, with love and compassion, is the path of Zen. Although sounding simple and obvious, living with the naturalness of our original nature is difficult, and requires training and concentrated attention. The process is noted in a famous Zen saying:

> Before you study Zen, mountains are mountains and rivers are rivers; while you are studying Zen, mountains are no longer mountains and rivers are no longer rivers; but once you have had enlightenment mountains are once again mountains and rivers again rivers.

Enlightenment consists of becoming what we already are from the beginning. As with another famous Zen metaphor, it's like riding an ox in search of an ox.

Before I studied Zen, mountains were mountains and rivers were rivers. After studying Zen, for some time I saw mountains and rivers as something other than mountains and rivers. But eventually, with more study and practice, I again saw mountains and rivers just as mountains and rivers. One begins with thoughtless being; then thinks and reasons thoughtfully; and with practice, returns to thoughtless being, seeing things with original nature. The return to thoughtless — now enlightened — being does not necessarily follow the middle stage of thought. But practice may bring the perfection of Zen. Beyond the constructions of thought, we may see things clearly, naturally as they are.

Eventually realized is the interdependence of all things, the selfless existence of everything. Also called "emptiness" in the sutras, mountains and rivers, as with all things, are dependent on all things in their origination. With enlightened mind and eyes, mountains and rivers are seen directly, beyond the blinders of thought and discourse. Zen practice is about returning to the ground of our natural being, realizing what we were born with and what is already waiting to be realized in the course of a life. We live in the present, relative reality, but know that in absolute reality everything originates dependently. A few years ago, in the course of a life, on a sunny afternoon, I watched the Dalai Lama approach as the crowd gathered at Deer Park.

Shunryu Suzuki would tell of mountains and rivers, about perceiving them before and after studying Zen. We are reminded by

John Cage in one of his indeterminacy stories, with music, that once Suzuki was asked, "What is the difference between before and after." He responded, "No difference, only the feet are a little bit off the ground." When the absolute realm has been glimpsed, and remembered, one lives with greater spontaneity and naturalness. Clothes are less heavy and one's step is lighter to the ground.

Right perception is my wish this first day of my seventy-ninth year. I'll walk about today lightly clad with feet a bit off the ground. All is in bloom — lilac, crab apple, sand cherry, and dogwood. An offering placed early in the morning on the lawn awaits red fox. A birthday, knowing that relatively every day is a new beginning. And knowing ultimately, absolutely, that there is no-birth and no-death. Today I celebrate this relative birthday, a reality shared with generations before and after.

Many times, when walking together or visiting each other in our homes, Bruce and I would ask each other, "What do you know for sure?" Trained as a biologist, Bruce von Zellen brought together the seemingly disparate teachings of science and the spiritual wisdom of Buddhism. He came to Buddhism the way most of us in the West come to it: out of need. How are we to bring some balance to our restless, inquisitive minds, especially ones trained to achieve and to excel?

The course thus was set in our explorations. Bruce would continue to remind us, following Krishnamurti, that the way is a pathless way. Stay close to the moment; our only reality is in the here and now. Take good care of the moment, and all will be well. But then Bruce would add, "There are no *shoulds* and no *oughts*." We recited the lines of the *Dhammapada* often: "All that we are is a result of what we have thought."

Bruce and I often discussed the latest finding or speculation from astrophysics, cosmology, cellular biology, or medical research. Bruce would expound with great delight on a report in the morning's *New York Times*. On other days, he would say firmly, "Richard, it's just thought." We read together Seung Sahn's book *Only Don't Know*. The phrase "only don't know" became one of our understandings together. And it was always good for a laugh.

We would read and talk about the writings of Alan Watts and the poetry of the Taoists. We read aloud the Zen poetry of Ryōkan:

> My hut lies in the middle of a dense forest;
> Every year the green ivy grows longer.
> No news of the affairs of men,
> Only the occasional song of a woodcutter.
> The sun shines and I mend my robe;
> When the moon comes out I read Buddhist poems.
> I have nothing to report, my friends.
> If you want to find the meaning, stop chasing after
> so many things.

I have heard it said that we live as long as we are remembered. Bruce passed away several years ago. I delivered the eulogy at his memorial service knowing that any celebration was just another way to mourn. I noted that I would rather be at other places on that day: driving west with Bruce over the Illinois prairie on our way to the Trappist monastery in Iowa. We would be listening to a tape of Jack Teagarden playing Duke Ellington's "Sophisticated Lady." Or we might be listening to a CD of Stan Getz playing the tenor saxophone on "I Can't Get Started," "Stella by Starlight," and "I Thought about You." On a Saturday evening, our families might be together by candlelight around the dinner table. From the beginning of my time with Bruce, I knew that I was witnessing an extraordinary life, one cloaked in the ordinariness of the everyday life. One thing I know for certain, Bruce is well remembered to this day.

A road trip yesterday down to Elkhorn to visit the staff at the Walworth County Historical Society and to look again at some of the family albums that we deposited in the archives after clearing out the farmhouse several years ago. I was given a tour of the newly acquired building that is being called the Heritage Center. And I walked again through the rooms of the Webster House.

The hymn "Sweet By and By" was written in this house by Joseph P. Webster in 1865, with the lyrics by S. Fillmore Bennett. The well-known refrain:

> In the sweet by and by,
> We shall meet on that beautiful shore;

> In the sweet by and by,
> We shall meet on that beautiful shore.

There is a description of the writing of the hymn in the scrapbook of clippings saved by my great-aunt Kate. We are told that the hymn was written, words and music, in less than an hour and was inspired by a temporary fit of depression that overtook Webster. It is related that Webster went into the home of his friend Dr. Sanford F. Bennett in a most despondent mood. The doctor asked what was the trouble. "It is no matter, it will be all right by and by," was Webster's reply. This remark acted as a flash of inspiration to them both. Bennett immediately sat down and wrote out the verses and Webster composed the music on his violin. Less than an hour later they were singing the hymn with two friends.

Joseph Webster continued to teach music in Elkhorn, and wrote the song "Lorena," which became famous after the Civil War. My mother's mother was named Lorena, along with many other girls of the time. Late in the afternoon, after my visit to the Webster House, I made certain to pass the farmhouse where Lorena was born. The refrain of "Sweet By and By" still echoing in my head and heart.

A ring of the bell, and in the doorway appears a Jehovah's Witness. And we will have our midweek conversation, sitting comfortably in the living room, finding scripture to justify whatever the subject. This time our attention turns to cosmology, and the question of whether anything can come from nothing. Apparently the Bible says it's so; I think that was what we found.

I haven't had such conversations since the passing of my good friend and colleague Al Meyer. Born in Denmark, he was well versed in the existentialism of Kierkegaard, and his research as a physicist took him into the realm of quantum physics. We talked together for years, and he and his wife, Cele, gave Solveig and me comfort when I was ill and being treated for the blood disease. At the memorial service for Al, a few years later, I repeated some of the stories Al and I told each other as we waited by the railroad track for the train carrying atomic waste through town. Al had cautioned all his life against nuclear power, his protest grounded in the research he had done early in his career at Oak Ridge. At the service, I said that sometimes Al and I would greet each other: "How are things going?" with the other responding, "Things could be worse." I must have been trying to make the point that now I was feeling that things could not be worse.

We had talked, and even laughed a lot, by the tracks that day as we protested the transport of nuclear waste across the Illinois prairie. I have imagined that day as the two of us being like the vagrants in Samuel Beckett's *Waiting for Godot*. I remember the lone tree beside the train station. At the service, I noted another image: Pancho and Lefty in Townes van Zandt's song as sung by Willie Nelson and Merle Haggard. "Living on the road my friend," and later, "He only did what he had to do." The loaded train passed by and we demonstrators returned to our homes.

We had wondered, Al and I, what if the quantum physics of the subatomic world reached into our world? Al would tell the story of Schrödinger's Cat, the cat that had no separate existence until it appeared in an experiment. Something about the probability that nuclear decay will release the mechanism that holds the poison that will destroy the cat, the cat being both dead and alive at the same time. The Boy in Beckett's play asks, "What am I to tell Mr. Godot?" The vagrant Vladimir answers, "Tell him you saw us." That we exist, waiting to be seen.

We are clueless, I had to add, at the edge of the abyss, not really knowing what is happening. I repeated my mantra from the Diamond Sutra: "All things are like a dream." Life as we know it is a fantasy, an illusion, a shadow with no substance of its own. All things are like dewdrops, and life is like a flash of lightning. Even so, as we sat in our camp chairs waiting for the moving van to take us to another place, Al and Cele shared their time with us. Al and I were still talking about the meaning of life, about the mystery of our existence. That was existence enough, and fortunate were we to have it. We were alive and happy. It could have been worse.

Twenty-Seven
Once Upon a Summertime

OTHER SEASONS HAVE COME and gone and now we are slipping slowly into another summer. Garden soils are still too wet for planting, but all around foliage is green and lush and fast growing through the rainy days. How many summer beginnings do you recall? The calendar of your life may count many, but you remember clearly only a few, maybe only two or three or four. This one I will remember because of the attention I am giving it in this Zen daybook of mine. And perhaps this summer is all the sweeter being informed by a sense of a precious few.

This summer begins with the voice of June Christy singing "Once Upon a Summertime." Listen to this song by Johnny Mercer and Michel Legrand, recorded by Christy at the beginning of the summer of 1977, and you will remember how this summer of 2013 began. Each summer begins only once. What happens during that summer happens only once. Fortunate we are to be here, at this time, at the beginning of summer. Another summer, once in a lifetime.

A weekend of lost and found in the cabinet drawers filled with cards and letters accumulated over decades. Solveig is away in the East visiting family, and my time is suspended in thought and reverie. In the drawers are the cards from friends traveling, the notes written inside art cards, the holiday cards sent throughout the seasons, the notices for memorial services, the greetings from former students, the birthday cards and wishes from family and friends, the valentine cards of love, and the many cards from my daughters as they have made their lives after leaving home. There are inclusions of poems and photographs. And among the buried treasures are the cards sending a "thank you."

Thanking one another is the glue, the expression of love that holds our lives together. A "thank you" conveys appreciation for a deed or gift, or simply an appreciation for being. The last written note from my mother was in a thank you card that expressed all our time together: "Thank you for all the things you have done for me." This card of thanks I place on top of a bundle of cards tied with a ribbon.

These gathered cards will be evidence of lives and relationships. Who we were and how we lived will be known by other generations as long as these cards — these artifacts — remain. A long ago past, a past receding further each year, will be more knowable for those who will pass this way. Shards from our lives, cards saved and not otherwise lost.

As in a midsummer night's dream, spirits dance, fairies fall from the sky, creatures come out of the woods and dash across the lawn, and fireflies flash in the moist evening. And there are apparitions that are in the mind's eye as ghosts from the past. Ghosts that still haunt us, reminding us of the lives we have led and the choices we have made. Ghosts that continue to give meaning to our lives.

Thank You

My book of reflections covering several years of my life will appear, will be published, this summer. These were the years of living across the border in Illinois before this final move to Wisconsin. The inscription on the back cover of the book tells the story: *This book is a record of a life lived during the last years of the twentieth century. Eighteen years of my life, between 1983 and 2001, were spent on the northern edge of the tallgrass prairie of Illinois, where prairie land gives way to the glaciated hills of Wisconsin. Eventually I would cross the border to be near the family farm. These years at century's end could easily be imagined as the years of waiting for the call that would finally define my life. But let us think of them as a dynamic and vital time, even in the waiting. I was the explorer, with open mind and open heart, on a journey of uncertain destination. These were the years that I sought the sublime in words and images and in this everyday life of ours. These were the years of my life as a camera.*

Although my life is different now, I am still a seeker on a journey of uncertain destination. There is the mystery of life that unfolds each day. Fewer images come from my camera. Travels along paths, through wooded lots, and over country roads are bounded by health and age. My travels more often are close to home, but no less wondrous than travel to a far country. My far country is at home.

The summers when I was young have shaped all the summers of my life. It is like the first sounds of creation echoing though the billions of years of the expanding universe. I am aging one year at a time, with new experiences each year, but the passing years are imprinted with the first experiences of youth. My summers, even with my aging — especially with my aging — carry the sounds and elements of long ago.

Another summer, and I still have the thoughts and sensations learned a good portion of a century ago. The crops have been planted in the fields; the green tips of corn have emerged from the warming soil; and the fields of alfalfa, clover, and timothy are maturing for a first cutting. Hay will be loaded onto the wagons, pulled to the barn, and unloaded into the mow.

Following the haying season will come the long days of cutting and binding the grain. My brother and I will hitch the Oliver tractor to the grain binder, and all day long we will go over the oat field adjusting the levers of the cutting blade and releasing the bundles. I am wearing a dust mask, outfitted with a penlight battery, to alleviate my hay fever caused by the dusty grain. I likely will be complaining to my father that I am being worked too hard. As I drive the tractor over rough and hilly fields, I have visions of kids in town playing and loafing while I am working all day in the hot sun.

At the end of the summer, the threshing machine, owned and worked cooperatively with several farm neighbors, will be pulled to the field and placed south of the barn. One of my favorite photographs, taken by my mother with the Kodak box camera, shows the threshing machine, powered by the old tractor turning the long and twisted belt, blowing straw into the air and into the growing stack. One man is on the horse-drawn wagon, pitching grain bundles into the hopper of the thresher; another stands atop the enormous machine, tending the threshed oats. A white leghorn hen is in the lower left-hand corner of the photograph, the photograph that I will carefully view all the summers that will follow. A photograph that captured one fleeting moment in this fleeting world, a photograph that will hold my imagination, my dreams, over a lifetime.

So much of summertime is dreamtime. We live our days as if in a dream. The tomato plants, after the night of soft rain, are growing in the garden below my window.

The first sighting in years: a large flicker, vividly patterned. He hops over the lawn feasting in the anthills. A mourning dove walks along the rail of the balcony. And a shimmering midmorning sunlight falls to earth through the branches of the flowering locust tree.

Still in mind is the weekend performance by Joan Baez. For an encore, she sang her song about memories and diamonds and rust. "Well I'll be damned here comes your ghost again." Decades ago — light-years ago — and now the phone call will bring back the memories. If it is nostalgia, however vague, take the diamonds and leave the rust.

In the evening there is the reading of the letters that Eudora Welty and William Maxwell wrote to each other over the course of their adult lives. The collected letters, *What There Is to Say We*

Have Said, was given to me by my daughter, both of us longtime readers of these two writers. Prompting me this morning to read the last page of Welty's book *One Writer's Beginnings.* "The memory is a living thing — it too is in transit. But during its moment, all that is remembered joins and lives — the old and the young, the past and the present, the living and the dead." Welty notes that her life has been a sheltered life, yet: "A sheltered life can be a daring life as well. For all serious daring starts from within."

How much I enjoy, how much I need, this time at the table as a new week begins on a summer morning. Did I mention the calls of crow and robin? And the chipmunk that darts among the rocks at the edge of the garden?

I once made a little drawing of one of the most familiar sights that I remember from my growing up on the farm. How many times in those years did I look out the living room window of the farmhouse, looking directly west across the fields, to the farm of my cousin Gail Olson? All the seasons of the year, and all the times of the day, I knew that my cousin was nearby. Gail's grandmother Lizzie and my grandfather Will were sister and brother.

The mailbox, standing to this day, was a reminder that even out in the country we were connected to a larger world. So much depended on the mailbox and the coming of the mailman. A walk across the yard to the mailbox, late morning before lunch, was travel that lasted throughout the lives of my father and mother, and was what I knew of travel when young.

Do we not still wait for the delivery that will take us, however far or briefly, to another place? We savor the moments of transport — and of return.

I am reminded again, in my summer reading, of Vladimir Nabokov's opening sentence in his autobiography *Speak, Memory*: "The cradle rocks above an abyss, and common sense tells us that our existence is but a brief crack of light between two eternities of darkness." Nabokov then observes that we humans view the prenatal abyss with greater calm than the one we are heading for. But both eternities must be accepted by us. Nabokov gives us this: "Nature expects a full-grown man to accept the two black voids, fore and aft, as stolidly as he accepts the extraordinary visions in between. Imagination, the supreme delight of the immortal and the immature, should be limited. In order to enjoy life, we should not enjoy it too much." But enjoyment and happiness, here and now, in between, are what we hope for and seek on summer days like these.

Little reading of fiction this summer when reality, this dream of reality, is so interesting. Days come and go as if we are drifting on a vast sea. We imagine ourselves as the crew of Thor Heyerdahl's *Kon-Tiki* floating westward across the Pacific hoping to reach a Polynesian island. Moments of attention, certainly, but much time spent in the drifting without other plans and purposes.

Today I am beginning to read Eudora Welty's novel *The Optimist's Daughter*. Mainly to explore her reflections on the nature and role of memory. The adult daughter in the novel is thinking about her deceased father, and memories are coming back with hurt. "The memory can hurt, time and again — but in that may lie its final mercy. As long as it's vulnerable to the living moment, it lives for us, and while it lives, and while we are able, we can give it up its due." The past — memories from the past — is alive for us when it is, using Welty's intriguing phrase, "vulnerable to the living moment." My memories and I are vulnerable, this summer, to the living moment.

Autobiographical writing is surrender to one's life. Autobiography, by its very definition, writes David Shields, "is concerned with the consciousness of its creator in the process of creating a self." But yet, I know that this writing, in the attention that I give to my days, is an attempt to create a self in the face of an ultimate reality where there is no self that is separate from everything else. In the end, as well as the time in between, the true self interpenetrates and is indistinguishable from all other energy and matter. This realization, this enlightenment, transcends the vulnerability of the living moment.

"But here in the real world," as the country singer Alan Jackson sings, "it's not that easy at all." In this relative reality, this created dream world, far from the realm of the absolute, some kind of self, distinguished and separated, is needed in order to function as a living human being. This takes courage, stamina, and understanding, and the ability to face daily the decisions to be made and the uncertainty of the consequences. Our vulnerability to the living moment is satisfied in the dreams for another day.

I will end this day of wandering, indoors and out, a day of shifting consciousness and thought, and emerging and fading self, with songs from Willie Nelson's album *Tougher Than Leather*. And I will listen carefully to the lines, this one for certain: "Never draw when you're facing the sun." Yes, here in the real world.

Twenty-Eight
Our Revels Now Are Ended

It is the middle of July of the year 2013. More than a year has passed since I began writing about this world of dreams. Did the blade of the diamond cut through the illusions, through the constructions of reality that appear to us as dreams? Our spiritual enlightenment is the awareness of this dream world. This awareness is itself enlightenment. We are the masters, the shepherds, of our dreaming.

The storyteller must end this telling of tales once again. We have conjured a year's worth of stories, tales that mark as well the life of the storyteller. We have inhabited a dream world and, as Prospero does in Shakespeare's *The Tempest,* declare, "Our revels now are ended."

We throw the book of tales to the sea. In this relative reality of a dream world, we know the impermanence of our existence and the mortality of our lives. Prospero imagines that our lives are dreams that fade into nothing.

> We are such stuff
> As dreams are made on, and our little life
> Is rounded with a sleep.

All this is true in this relative world of dreams. But, yet, remember the fruit of this year's quest: an absolute realm lies beyond our dreams, perhaps. In the meantime we are shepherds of our dreams, tellers of tales we share with others, and keepers of the wonders of our existence here on earth. We give thanks for this stage on which we move and have our being. And we have hopes for the revels of another day.

Illustrations

PAGE

- 8 The Old Place
Richard Quinney
- 16 A Man with Horses
Unknown
- 24 Quinney Family Farm
Richard Quinney
- 30 Bridget O'Keefe Quinney
M. B. Barton
- 35 John Quinney Visiting Neighbors
Unknown
- 42 Lorena Taylor Holloway
Alice Holloway
- 55 Bedrock, Jens Jensen Children's Park
Richard Quinney
- 66 Sleigh and Horse
Unknown
- 71 Will and Mabel Holloway
Unknown
- 79 Valentine from Great-Aunt Kate
Unknown
- 88 Richard Quinney with Holstein Heifer
Alice Holloway Quinney
- 99 Great Gray Owl in Middleton
Eloisa Callender
- 105 The Marsh
Richard Quinney

115 Marjorie Quinney
 Unknown
134 Thank You Card
 Unknown
139 Mailbox at the Farm
 Richard Quinney

Bibliography

Bashō, Matsuo. *A Haiku Journey: Bashō's Narrow Road to a Far Province.* Tr. Dorothy Britton. New York: Kodansha International, 2002.

Bashō, Matsuo. *Narrow Road to the Interior and Other Writings.* Ed. Sam Hamill. Boston: Shambhala, 2000.

Bernanos, Georges. *The Diary of a Country Priest.* Trans. Pamela Morris. New York: Carroll & Graf, 1983.

Burkhardt, Barbara. *William Maxwell: A Literary Life.* Urbana: University of Illinois Press, 2005.

Cage, John. *Silence: Lectures and Writings.* Middletown, CT: Wesleyan University Press, 1961.

Calhoun, Charles C. *Longfellow: A Rediscovered Life.* Boston: Beacon Press, 2004.

Cook, Francis H. *Sounds of Valley Streams: Enlightenment in Dōgen's Zen.* Albany: State University of New York Press, 1989.

Eliot, T. S. *The Complete Poems and Plays of T. S. Eliot.* London: Faber and Faber, 1969.

Flanagan, John T. "Thoreau in Minnesota," *Minnesota History* 16 (March 1935): 35–46.

Greenblatt, Stephen. *The Swerve: How the World Became Modern.* New York: W. W. Norton, 2011.

Grumbach, Doris. *Fifty Days of Solitude.* Boston: Beacon Press, 1994.

Hamill, Sam, and J. P. Seaton, eds. *The Poetry of Zen.* Boston: Shambhala, 2004.

Hanh, Thich Nhat. *The Diamond That Cuts Through Illusion: Commentaries on the Prajnaparamita Sutra Diamond Sutra.* Berkeley, CA: Parallax Press, 2010.

Hanh, Thich Nhat. *The Heart of Understanding: Commentaries on the Prajnaparamita Heart Sutra.* Berkeley, CA: Parallax Press. 2009.

Hanh, Thich Nhat. *No Death, No Fear: Comforting Wisdom for Life.* New York: Riverhead Books, 2002.

Hanh, Thich Nhat. *Touching the Earth: 46 Guided Meditations for Mindfulness Practice.* Berkeley, CA: Parallax Press, 2008.

Hardwick, Elizabeth. *Sleepless Nights.* New York: Random House, 1979.

Hemingway, Ernest. *A Moveable Feast.* New York: Scribner, 1964.

Hill, Robert W., ed. *Tennyson's Poetry.* New York: W. W. Norton, 1999.

Inman, Arthur Crew. *The Inman Diary: A Public and Private Confession,* vols. 1–2. Ed. Daniel Aaron. Cambridge, MA: Harvard University Press, 1985.

Irmscher, Christoph. *Longfellow Redux.* Urbana: University of Illinois Press, 2006.

Loori, John Daido. *Two Arrows Meeting Mid-Air: The Zen Koan.* Boston: Charles E. Tuttle, 1994.

Maezumi, Hakuyu Taizan. *The Way of Everyday Life.* Los Angeles: Zen Center of Los Angeles, 1978.

Marrs, Suzanne, ed. *What There Is to Say We Have Said: The Correspondence of Eudora Welty and William Maxwell.* Boston: Houghton Mifflin Harcourt, 2011.

Nāgārjuna and Kaysang Gyatso. *The Precious Garland and the Song of the Four Mindfulnesses.* Trans. and ed. Jeffrey Hopkins, Lati Rimpoche, and Anne Klein. London: G. Allen and Unwin, 1975.

Niven, Penelope. *Thornton Wilder: A Life.* New York: HarperCollins, 2012.

North, Sterling. *Hurry, Spring!* New York: E. P. Dutton, 1966.

North, Sterling. *The Wolfling: A Documentary Novel of the Eighteen-Seventies.* New York: E. P. Dutton, 1969.

Pythagorean Sangha. *The Diamond Sutra with Supplemental Texts.* Ed. Raghavan Iyer. Santa Barbara, CA: Concord Grove Press, 1983.

Quinney, Richard. *A Sense Sublime.* Madison, WI: Borderland Books, 2013.

Red Pine. *The Diamond Sutra: The Perfection of Wisdom.* Berkeley, CA: Counterpoint, 2001.

Ricks, Christopher. *Tennyson*. New York: Macmillan, 1972.
Salter, James. *All That Is*. New York: Alfred A. Knopf, 2013.
Shakespeare, William. *The Riverside Shakespeare*. 2nd ed. Ed. G. Blakemore Evans and J. J. M. Tobin. Boston: Houghton and Mifflin, 1996.
Shields, David, *Enough about You: Adventures in Autobiography*. New York: Simon & Schuster, 2002.
Stryk, Lucien. *And Still Birds Sing: New and Selected Poems*. Athens, OH: Swallow Press, 1998.
Suzuki, Shunryu. *Zen Mind, Beginner's Mind*. New York: Weatherhill, 1982.
Teale, Edwin Way. *North with the Spring*. New York: Dodd, Mead, 1951.
Tennyson, Charles. *Alfred Tennyson*. New York: Macmillan, 1949.
Vinz, Mark. *Long Distance*. Fairwater, WI: MWPH Books, 2005.
Welty, Eudora. *One Writer's Beginnings*. Cambridge, MA: Harvard University Press, 1984.
Welty, Eudora. *The Optimist's Daughter*. New York: Random House, 1972.

A NOTE ABOUT THE AUTHOR

Richard Quinney was born and raised on a farm in Wisconsin. He is the author of several books of nonfiction — memoirs and spiritual meditations — and books of photographs, as well as works in the field of sociology. He has held professorships at the University of Kentucky, Northern Illinois University, and New York University. He is the recipient of the Erich Fromm Award, the Edwin H. Sutherland Award, and the August Derleth Award for his book *Things Once Seen,* and a Fulbright Award for research and teaching in Ireland. He lives in Madison, Wisconsin.

A NOTE ON COMPOSITION AND PRINTING

This book was typeset in Minion Pro, a digital typeface designed by Robert Slimbach in 1990 for Adobe Systems. The name comes from the traditional naming system for type sizes, in which minion is between nonpareil and brevier. It is inspired by late Renaissance-era type. The paper is 70 lb. Accent Opaque Smooth Warm White.

The book was designed by Ken Crocker and printed by Worzalla Publishing.